The Story of the
Mexican War

BOOKS BY COLONEL RED REEDER

With NARDI REEDER CAMPION

The Story
of the Mexican War

by COLONEL RED REEDER

Illustrated by Frederick Chapman

MEREDITH PRESS   New York

First edition

Library of Congress Catalog Card Number: 67-18498

MANUFACTURED IN THE UNITED STATES OF AMERICA FOR MEREDITH PRESS

VAN REES PRESS • NEW YORK

CONTENTS

MAPS

Maps are by the author and Edward J. Krasnoborski

The Story of the
Mexican War

1   DANGEROUS TERRITORY

THE hot Texas sun beat down on the marching men as if it were a pile driver. The heat and the loose sand made the trail seem like the road to hell. The straps of the packs bit into the shoulders of the men like medieval instruments of torture. Almost as if they were marching in their sleep, the Regulars in the column plodded along. As for the newly joined recruits, they felt each step would be their last. There was no letup. "Keep going!" the sergeants said.

This was a march that would be damned or applauded in the States. It would cause stormy debates. Some held it was overdue; others said it was a drive to help slavery.

Only a few soldiers fell out to the side of the trail. The sixty-two-year-old general on a white horse had been up and down the column all morning. His presence—a nod here and there, once in a while a word to an officer or a noncom—proved a friendly spur. Now, on the only knoll in sight, the general sat carelessly in the saddle. A blue gingham coat covered his powerful torso. Clapped on his head sat a wide-brimmed yellow straw hat. Gen. Zachary Taylor looked like a farmer.

In the middle of the long line a color sergeant carried the flag, thirteen stripes and twenty-eight stars. This was 1846, and the column marching into disputed territory expected trouble from Mexicans. Both sides claimed Texas.

One thought buoyed the US soldiers: The general in command was experienced—thirty-eight years in the Regular Army. The men knew he was brave. He had proved that in the War of 1812 when he fought Indians in Indiana and Illinois Territories and in Florida. There was no doubt Zachary Taylor was fearless. He lacked education, but he had a know-how of his own.

The soldiers realized the chance they were taking. Every step put them closer to trouble. There was a joke they kept using in one form or another, over and over. A recruit tried his hand: "Sergeant, we're annexation bait, ain't we?"

The sergeant snorted, "Maybe. Don't worry about it. Close up. Try to keep step. Makes the going easier."

Capt. William S. Henry of New York, one of the young West Point officers riding in the long column, twisted in his saddle and called to the infantrymen behind him, "Fourteen miles to the next stream. The scouts say in a little while we'll be walking on clay. It'll be easier."

That morning the soldiers had hiked through Texas country resembling a garden, across acres of wild pea and fields of blue bonnets. Now thickets of bushy mesquite and clumps of scrub oak dotted the landscape. This was ambush country.

The 1846 woolen uniform of the United States infantry helped make the march a torture. Light blue coats had become dusty gray. Horseshoe blanket rolls looped over the left shoulders made sure that not a wisp of air moved in or out. White crossbelts helped the blanket rolls. The blue caps ballooned like the tops of mushrooms. This was a European type, parade-ground uniform. In 1846 armies fought in their best formal wear.

Black leather cartridge boxes, stamped U.S., loaded with ammunition, ate into the small of the soldiers' backs; each foot soldier carried forty rounds. Long muzzle-loading muskets weighing nine pounds twelve ounces, and spearlike bayonets, almost eleven ounces, completed the burden. Some companies shouldered the new Hall flintlock rifle, a breech loader. Hardly a canteen in the infantry contained more than a few swallows of warm water.

The men envied Captain Henry riding a horse. To the foot soldiers he appeared almost like a man from another planet. His sword, swinging easily in its scabbard under the tassel of a red sash, was more than a symbol of authority. It was sharp.

On the eleventh day of the hike out of Corpus Christi, Texas—March 19, 1846—a wild blast of bugles in front of the column startled the soldiers. Thousands of plovers darted up from sparse prairie grass and flew for the horizon. From the front came the signal, "Halt!"

A US dragoon, on a chestnut horse covered with sweat, galloped for the rear past Henry's company. The sunburned face of the mounted infantryman contrasted with the blue of his tight-fitting coat. A yellow band around his blue cap looked like a man-made halo.

"What's up?" Captain Henry yelled.

The dragoon reined his horse to a halt. "Thirty Mexicans

with a piece of paper," called the dragoon. "Where's General Taylor, sir?"

"Back with the wagon train."

The dragoon spurred the animal and headed for the three hundred wagons. (There was approximately one wagon for every ten soldiers.)

The "piece of paper" from the Mexicans warned General Taylor and his men to leave the country. It accused the United States of treachery in annexing Texas and said if the column proceeded the result would be war. The paper bore the signature of a Mexican general, who said that not far away he had four thousand soldiers.

The peculiar lines cupping Taylor's mouth deepened; he pocketed the message and signaled, *Forward!* The band struck up "Yankee Doodle." The sergeant harped at recruits, "Come on! Pick up step." The Mexicans disappeared in a cloud of dust. A breeze from the Gulf rippled out the American flag.

Then Taylor ordered a battery of artillery into position where it could fire—just in case. In Indian country he had seen ambush in territory like this.

The general felt unsure about artillery, especially the new-fangled horse-drawn cannons. Oxen could outpull horses, even if oxen plodded along at only a mile and a half an hour. Nor did Taylor like artillery officers with their fancy red stripes down their trousers' legs—drones, he called them. Neither was he entranced with the young West Point officers. School officers, some termed them. But Capt. Charles F. Smith, West Point artilleryman from Pennsylvania, talked very convincingly about "his" guns. He trotted alongside the four artillery companies like a mother hen.

The bronze cannons, barrels polished bright yellow, flashed like mirrors. They bumped along on fifty-four inch wheels, each gun totaling 1,784 pounds. The question bothering Gen. Zachary Taylor was, "How good can they shoot?"

"They can hit a target up to twelve hundred yards," Captain Smith had assured him.

To Taylor, this seemed unnecessarily long range, maybe too long. Infantry won battles, not big guns.

It took courage to be an infantryman—you fixed your three-cornered bayonet on the end of your rifle and closed with the enemy. With a well-trained man behind the gun, a flintlock musket could be depended upon up to three hundred yards. The newer Hall rifle, caliber .52 breech loader, could not reach out at a greater range, but you went through fewer steps to fire. They drilled you in the thirteen motions to fire the musket until you were dizzy. No step could be slighted. For instance, Step Number Eight required you to return the ramrod to its place beneath the barrel after you rammed the ball home, and if you forgot, when you ran to a new position, you could not shoot.

The march ground southward at 2 ½ miles an hour. In spite of the brilliant uniforms, the trek along the Gulf of Mexico was drab. Clouds drifting in just overhead seemed to mirror the flatness of the land.

General Taylor had his orders from President James K. Polk. His message was, "March to the bank of the Rio Grande as soon as convenient."

President Polk was gambling. The United States had a total of but 5,300 soldiers, scattered over one hundred posts. Now over half of its army, marching into territory claimed by both countries, could be expected to dig up trouble.

Taylor's entry into the disputed territory acted as a goad to the Mexicans.

When the general neared the mouth of the Rio Grande, he rested his three thousand soldiers for a day to make sure that the US Navy had unloaded enough supplies at Point Isabel before he hiked deeper into the disputed territory.

When his column reached a point twenty-six miles by road from the mouth of the Rio Grande, the soldiers saw a town that to them looked like Paris. It stood less than two hundred yards away across the yellow river. They had expected a

border town with buildings of adobe clay, but they found a village two miles square, laid out "with beauty and precision," centering around an unfinished cathedral. However, when scouts reported, "There are four thousand Mexican soldiers in or near Matamoros," the town suddenly seemed like a trap.

Crossing the Rio Grande in a flat boat under protection of a white flag, came Gen. Romulo Vega. He protested politely but vigorously to Taylor's assistant, General Worth. Vega, in his white trousers, blue coat faced in red and crowned with yellow epaulets, and fore-and-aft hat trimmed with white feathers, looked like an admiral-of-the-sea from the previous century. But there was nothing funny about General Vega of Mexico. He was angry.

"Haughty Bill" Worth listened. When the Mexican leader stopped, Worth snapped, "The United States Army is here to stay," and the conference failed.

Meanwhile, across the river near thatched huts bordering the town, the Mexicans labored to improve their defenses. They hated the presence of the American soldiers on the Rio Grande.

Taylor on the north bank, taking no chances, ordered an old-fashioned plainsman's camp with the wagons parked in circles. Within the rings the soldiers removed their packs, tossed off their crossbelts, spread their blankets, and tried to get comfortable. Out beyond the campfires walked the sentinels.

Taylor listened to Gen. William Jenkins Worth, then said, "In the morning, let's have these young West Point engineers build us a strong fort and put some cannons in it."

You could feel the hot breath of war.

2   "FIFTEEN DEAD"

THE next morning the Americans raised a flagpole as if to prove the area was theirs.

Haughty Bill Worth saluted General Taylor and claimed the honor of raising the Stars and Stripes, and Taylor approved. The ranks presented arms. Officers' swords flashed in salute. The band played "The Star-Spangled Banner" as Worth hauled away. On the red, white, and blue flag the morning sun highlighted the colors.

Standing beside him was his rival, David Twiggs. It was Worth versus Twiggs, and even the lowest private knew it.

General Twiggs, severe and as pompous as Squire Trelawney in *Treasure Island*, bore the nickname Old Davy the Bengal Tiger. Back at Corpus he had had men lashed for smuggling whiskey into camp, and once he had the surgeon horsewhipped. Powerfully built, six feet tall with a thick red face, red hair, and whiskers, Twiggs looked like God's angry man, and he had a violent temper and a barbed tongue. Men avoided him—he stood for iron discipline.

Rank was the cause of the argument between the two generals. Worth thought his brevet rank (temporary rank awarded in place of a medal) placed him above Davy the Bengal Tiger. Worth, the better soldier of the two, had been a commandant of cadets under Colonel Thayer at West Point. This school, established in 1802, had been operating forty-four years. It was the only technical and engineering school in the United States. Now, if there was to be war, the Military Academy had young leaders ready.

The officers building Fort Texas told stories about Haughty Bill Worth. It was customary in his time as commandant at West Point to allow cadets to drink on Christmas Day and on the Fourth of July. So that he would not be embarrassed, the "Supe," Col. Sylvanus Thayer, left the post one Fourth. But when he walked back up the hill from a steamboat in the Hudson, he saw a mass of cadets sweep by with Haughty Bill Worth on their shoulders. This time, Thayer asked no questions.

General Worth understood people better than General Twiggs, but the argument over rank blinded Worth. Old Rough and Ready (the newswriters' and the soldiers' nickname for Zachary Taylor) sidestepped the argument over who ranked whom and sent papers about the quarrel to Gen. Winfield Scott in Washington. "Let him make the decision," Taylor said.

Four weeks passed as the two armies faced one another across the yellow Rio Grande. In the evening señoritas from

Matamoros swam in the river, sometimes without clothes. Word came across that each American soldier who joined the Mexican Army would be given 320 acres of land. Americans swam the river each night—deserters—and some drowned. One of the men who joined the Mexican Army was Sgt. John Riley. Perhaps he deserted because he detested hard discipline.

Taylor hated to lose Riley, an expert artilleryman, because he could help the Mexicans. The Matamoros *Gazette* wrote: "Forty-three men and six slaves have left the barbarians. We expect momentarily *Old Taylor, body and soul.*"

Bad news for General Worth arrived from Washington. The argument over rank had been decided by the President himself, who ruled in favor of General Twiggs. The sensitive Worth left for Washington in a huff, his reputation suffering because he departed at a time of danger.

In mid-April, 1846, excitement shook the Mexican town of Matamoros. Capt. William Henry wrote in his diary: "A salute of 20 guns was fired, the church bells rang, the bands played, the troops arrived." Word drifted across the Rio Grande that the celebration honored General Ampudia. Taylor knew about the new leader, who had spent part of his life in Cincinnati and enjoyed a reputation for bravery.

Ampudia's first act was to send "Don Z. Taylor" a letter headed "God and Liberty." It told Taylor he had twenty-four hours to start his march back. Taylor sent a note saying he was in camp by order of President Polk and that his orders permitted no withdrawal.

There was a stalemate, but life was exciting because danger in the form of guerrillas ringed the US camp. The Texas Rangers respected the guerrillas. "They don't have uniforms," the rangers said, "but they can fight harder than some Mexican regiments." Col. Trueman Cross either was careless or he did not believe in the ferocity of the guerrillas. One evening he sauntered out beyond the ring of sentinels. Guerrillas seized him, stripped him of his uniform, and banged him over the head with the butt of a pistol. General Twiggs commanded the funeral escort, and they buried Cross at the foot of the flagstaff.

When a large force of Mexicans crossed the river, General Taylor ordered out a party of dragoons to find out what was up. They rode out of camp, a jaunty group—sixty-eight of them—Capt. Seth Thornton in command. At his side rode Capt. William Hardee of Camden County, Georgia, eight years out of West Point.

About twelve miles below the camp, near a ranch, the dragoons spotted a large group of Mexicans. Thornton held up his hand—the signal *Halt!* At this moment the dragoons looked behind and saw they were surrounded. The figures vary: The Mexicans numbered between 1,600 and 2,400, reports said later.

The dragoons galloped into a circle. A Mexican lancer in a red coat came forward with a demand that Captain Thornton surrender. He shook his head and while the lancer was riding back Thornton called to his men: "Let's cut our way out!"

It was slaughter. Fifteen Americans died in this fight on the banks of the Rio Grande. The rest were either wounded or captured. It looked for a while as if Captains Thornton and Hardee would escape, but Thornton, who was badly hurt, became a captive not far from the American camp. Hardee and a few others headed for the river with an idea of swimming it and returning later, but they mired down in a swamp. They prepared to sell their lives dearly.

A Mexican officer persuaded them to surrender, promising they would be treated honorably as prisoners of war. The

Mexicans kept their word and then some. General Ampudia invited the captured officers to live with him in Matamoros, and they ate at his table.

The day after the fight the Mexicans sent a wounded dragoon to General Taylor in an oxcart with information about the scrap. A poorly worded but polite note informed the American general that his opponents lacked a "flying hospital," but that those of Thornton's patrol who had survived "would be treated with the rights of prisoners of war."

This was April 26, 1846. Taylor sent a hurried note to Washington giving the details. He asked the governors of Louisiana and Texas to rush volunteers. It was obvious the war had started.

3   BACKGROUND: DISTRUST, HATRED, AND REBELLION

WHAT caused the war?

For over a century many writers, in describing the unusual Mexican War, pictured the United States as a villain who fought Mexico. What are the facts?

Even officers in the United States Army felt their country was in the wrong. In 1846 no system existed in the army to inform soldiers on topics of the day. Many had only hazy ideas of national problems.

Some of the best minds in the United States—for instance, Sen. John Milton Miles of Connecticut—thought that fighting Mexico was in the interests of humanity. Many citizens believed otherwise. The issue is still debatable.

The causes lie in frictions between Texas settlers and Mexicans; in the behavior of an unstable Mexican government, ruled at times by a cruel dictator; in border warfare; in the annexation of Texas; in the desire of Mexican leaders to fight the United States; and on top of it all the aggressiveness of a President, James Polk, who supplied the spark igniting the explosive situation.

Texas has an unusual and rousing story. Before its record began, fearless Franciscans and Jesuits rode burros into the land from Spanish settlements in the south, and built churches and missions. Many friars paid with their lives for the crimes of the military adventurers who made slaves of the Indians.

In 1528 Cabeza de Vaca, intrepid explorer from Spain, had his barges wrecked on the Texas coast near Galveston. He and three survivors, one a Moorish slave, escaped. During their travels they saw the buffalo, the wide country of West Texas, and maybe part of California. Because Vaca and his companions made the sign of the Cross when they worked to heal a sick Indian, they were regarded as mystics.

Other Spaniards came, and they built forts as well as missions. Then French explorers arrived. More adventurers, out for gold, silver, and everything they could get, raided Indian settlements. Pirates and smugglers, such as Jean Lafitte, and Mexican revolutionists inhabited Galveston Island. Fear of French rivalry made the Spanish grasp the region.

Under the lash of hard times in Missouri, in 1820, Moses Austin of Connecticut rode his horse to San Antonio, Texas, where he sought the Spanish governor Martínez. The Yankee said, "I request permission to bring three hundred of the best families to Texas."

"How will they make a living, señor?"

"We will farm, sir. Cotton, tobacco, sugarcane, and corn."

Because Moses Austin was a compelling man, and because the governor was interested in Americans who wanted to become loyal Spanish citizens, he approved. Austin rode back to Missouri to await his answer from the Spanish government, but before word came he died.

When permission arrived, young Stephen Austin, influenced by his father's enthusiasm for Texas, brought in the next year three hundred families to the fertile, well-watered country bordering the Gulf. Wild Indians were a menace, but the settlers held on and helped one another.

Austin, an outstanding nonmilitary leader and a diplomat with a gentle disposition, worked to get along with the Mexicans, but not all of the Americans felt as Austin, "the Father of Texas," did. Some talked in a condescending manner to the Mexicans—maybe this was the beginning of the trouble.

A little over a year after he arrived in Texas, Stephen Austin rode horseback to San Antonio to report to the governor. To his amazement, Austin discovered that Mexico had revolted against Spain. The governor, not sure of his own standing, shrugged his shoulders and advised Austin to ride further, to Mexico City, to make sure his permit to settle was still valid. Austin felt disappointed, but he faced the dangerous twelve-hundred-mile journey with a few companions, disguised as beggars to fool highwaymen.

They found the Mexican government a madhouse. Because of the confusion and turmoil, it took Austin more than a year to have his grant confirmed but he made good use of his time as he waited: He learned the Spanish language and studied the Mexicans.

When he arrived back in his colony, he found that some settlers, completely discouraged, had returned to the United

States. Now more powerful than ever, he parceled out the land, 177 acres to a farmer and more to men who brought settlers to Texas. In ten years over five thousand settlers lived in Texas.*

It was hard going. One Texan said, "Texas is a great place for men and dogs, but it's a mighty bad place for women and oxen." The men found time to hunt, but for the pioneer woman there was little save work, work, work.

The Mexicans observed that many colonists sent their children back to the United States for education, and in the delicate matter of religion, large numbers of the newcomers were not as expected: They were Roman Catholics in name only. "These *hombres*," the Mexicans told one another, "look to the day when they hope Texas will be part of the United States."

Neither side understood the other. Texans admired Mexican horsemanship and the beautiful silver-appointed saddles and bridles. The Mexicans liked the way the *norteamericanos* made their farms produce and the way they fought the Indians—but that was all. Arguments sprang up over land, the Mexicans claiming acres the pioneers had developed. Although the settlers thought they needed slaves, the Mexicans abolished slavery in Texas in 1829. Years later slavery in Texas became an important point in the turmoil that led to the war with Mexico.

In 1830 the Mexicans passed a law limiting the number of Americans coming to Texas. It also sent convicts to build roads and to make their homes in Texas. It stationed soldiers among the settlers and slapped taxes on incoming goods—unless they were made in Mexico. All this heaped pine knots on

* See Map No. 2, page 19.

the fires of the quarrel. It made the Texans feel like most of the American colonists of 1776.

Fighting broke out between the two sides, near the mouth of the Brazos.

Two years after the tax law placed a halter on the pioneers, one of the most amazing Americans of his time rode his horse out of Oklahoma, across a ford in the Red River, and jogged on for about five hundred miles into Texas. This was Sam Houston, who became a legend in his day—a controversial one.

FIRST SETTLERS
on the Brazos and Colorado
near the Gulf
No. 2

His background is almost inconceivable. As a boy he had lived with the Cherokees, a chief adopting him as a son. The Indians called him "the Raven," and he liked that. At Horseshoe Bend in Alabama, during the War of 1812, he fought Creek Indians under General Jackson, receiving a barbed arrow in his intestines, and a musket blast almost tore off his right arm and shoulder. These wounds bothered him all of his life, but his bravery earned the staunch friendship of Andrew Jackson.

After five years' army service, Sam Houston resigned, maybe with some regret. He studied law, became a congressman from Tennessee and eventually its governor. He stood six feet two inches tall, but when he entered a room his dynamic personality made you think he was a giant. Luminous blue-gray eyes, a soft voice, and a courteous manner helped make him unusual. Perhaps he drank too much at times—the Cherokees gave him a new nickname, Big Drunk. Although vain and selfish, he was an effective, natural leader.

When he rode into Texas in 1832, he headed for San Antonio so he could make peace between "his" tribe and the dangerous Comanches. Houston was in and out of Texas, but when the settlers needed him, he helped them write the constitution they would use if they could pull away from Mexico.

When the Mexicans heard of this and of similar meetings, they said, "Now we *know* the Texans want to be a separate state." The boundaries of Texas were vague, but to lose the tremendous, fertile country would be a blow to Mexico.

On the pioneers' side, the law of 1830 felt like a yoke. To get rid of it they persuaded Stephen Austin to ride once again over the long trails to Mexico City. When he arrived, he found a revolution under way and people suffering from cholera. Even though he was on a peaceful mission, the Mexicans looked upon him as a schemer. They arrested him and tossed him into jail. For three months he suffered in a vile cell, incommunicado—no one could see him and he could send no messages.

Finally friends located him, but it took a year to secure his release. By the time he was back with his people, two years had passed. He found chaos. Mexican raiders made the border country a hell. Settlers were leaving their homes.

Austin knew the cause of the trouble. A powerful leader in Mexico City, who had toyed with him while he rotted in jail, felt happy to see the American pioneers suffer. This was Santa Anna, one of the most treacherous men of the first half of the nineteenth century.

He was the scourge of the Mexican people, off and on for thirty years, as well as a two-faced American enemy. Santa Anna could be charming when he wanted, but he was untrustworthy and enjoyed intrigue. He would promise anything, with no idea of keeping his promise, if he thought he could gain. Soon after he rose to power he betrayed his countrymen by becoming a dictator. As President, he shared profits with crooked contractors who were paid to equip his soldiers. This Mexican leader sent an army to Texas to enforce the law.

The people of Texas were in danger because they were unprepared. To try to remedy the desperate situation, they elected Austin—an inspirational but not a military leader—general of their newly formed little army. He said, "I will wear myself out by inches rather than submit to Santa Anna."

But suddenly the pioneers decided that Austin and two others should travel to Washington to get help from the United States. A stout-looking Texan, Indian fighter Edward Burleson, was elected as the army's head.

A Mexican deserter brought word to Burleson that many

soldiers in the Mexican Army in San Antonio felt discouraged. When one of the Texas colonels, handsome Ben Milam, heard this, he shouted at the volunteers, "Who will go with old Ben Milam into San Antonio?" The revolt of the Texans started. This was December, 1835.

In San Antonio for four days and nights it was tooth, nail, and claw. Many homes and buildings were wrecked. This was an unusual victory: about 350 Texans defeated approximately sixteen hundred Mexicans. The Texans lost only two men, but one of these was "old Ben Milam."

In January of the next year, Santa Anna sent his armies back to Texas. He directed his well-organized force while riding at the tail of one of the columns in a buckboard pulled by six white mules. Close by, on the flanks, trotted fifty expert cavalrymen, his bodyguards. Behind lumbered his personal baggage train and crates of selected chickens—fighting cocks.

Not only did Santa Anna's forces outnumber the Texans, the odds in his favor increased when many Texans, including General Burleson, left to tend their families and homes. There was confusion as to who was in command and who would give orders. Finally, Sam Houston was named commander-in-chief. Later he had his portrait painted as Marius, a Roman general of experience and skill who converted an assemblage of citizens into an army.

In the meantime, the Mexicans headed for San Antonio to attack the tiny garrison in the stone mission, the Alamo.

Within the walls of the Church of the Alamo were about 180 Texas rebels. Among the leaders were Davy Crockett, bear hunter, frontier politician, and story teller; James Bowie, one of the first to wear the knife by that name, a husky who had served with the fierce Apaches and who had spied on the

Mexicans; and a striking-looking red-headed lawyer from Alabama, Lt. Col. William Travis, commander of the Alamo.

The stage was set for a tragedy. Texas would lose brave men who could not be replaced and would gain a rallying cry and a tradition to hold forever.

4 BACKGROUND:
RISE OF THE TEXANS

WHEN scouts on top of the Alamo saw Santa Anna's hordes, the church bells rang. Texans tore for their battle stations. Loopholes, perhaps not enough of them, had been cut in the stone and adobe buildings that included a church, convent, hospital, barracks, and walled-in plaza. This plaza, 150 yards long by about fifty yards wide—a little larger than an American football field—Colonel Travis decided would be the main battleground. Along its south side the ancient wall had crumbled, and in its place the defenders had constructed a breastwork and two rows of palisades, but the place could hardly be called a fort.

On the evening of the second day of the siege, Colonel Travis asked a courier to slip through the lines to San Felipe,

150 miles to the west, with a letter. It bore the heading: "FEBY. 24TH, 1836. TO THE PEOPLE OF TEXAS AND ALL AMERICANS IN THE WORLD." The letter pleaded for help. It said that the Mexicans were bombarding the Alamo around the clock and had "demanded a surrender ... otherwise, the garrison are to be put to the sword if the fort is taken. I have answered ... with a cannon shot. ..."

On a nearby hill Santa Anna ran up a blood-red flag—symbol of no quarter. The Texans expected none, and they continued to fight, because they thought it their duty to gain time so Sam Houston could assemble men and organize an army.

For almost two weeks the weary Texans held out against approximately 2,400 Mexicans. No aid came. Finally, at President Santa Anna's order, bugles and bands played "El Degüello," ancient music from the days of Spanish wars against the wild Moors. It meant, "Beheading, cutting the throat ... no mercy to every opponent."

Brave Mexican soldiers, armed with axes, scaling ladders, knives, and rifles, rushed the mission and swarmed inside.

Mrs. Sue Dickinson, wife of Lieutenant Dickinson, was alone in the church with her infant daughter and a Negro servant of Colonel Travis. She wrote later of the terror:

The struggle lasted more than two hours, when my husband rushed into the church where I was with my child. He said, "Great God, Sue! The Mexicans are inside the walls!" ... Then with a parting kiss, he drew his sword and plunged into the strife. ... [Later] I saw four Mexicans toss him up in the air, as you would a bundle of fodder, with their bayonets, and then shoot him. ...

Vicious hand-to-hand fighting occurred as the defenders made their last stand. When it was finally over, about six hundred Mexicans lay dead. Only six Texans were left alive, and shortly they were cut to pieces at Santa Anna's order. To complete the bloody scene, the bodies of Travis, Bowie, and Crockett were tossed from bayonet to bayonet.

President Santa Anna cleaned up the place by ordering the corpses of the Texans—about 187 of them—stacked, soaked with oil, and burned. Two Negro slaves, women, and children were spared. The Mexican leader sent word of the massacre to Sam Houston by one of the surviving women, telling him this was the punishment he would deal out to the rest of the country.

While the Alamo was under siege, a convention of Texans on the Brazos River declared its independence.

On the heels of the Alamo catastrophe came news of another disaster. At Goliad, Texas, ninety miles southwest of San Antonio, Col. J. W. Fannin surrendered 475 men to a Mexican general, thinking they would be treated as prisoners of war. Santa Anna, believing these men to be filibusters (private adventurers), ordered their execution. A few escaped, but 390 were shot down in cold blood.

When news of the disasters reached the United States, many felt sympathy for the people of Texas. Thousands believed the time was not far away when Texas should be a state in the Union.

The entire Texas population now scurried eastward to escape the killer. Santa Anna's force, about three thousand strong, fanned out in pursuit. Panic developed. The settlers—including some Mexicans who considered themselves Texans—left farms, homes, ranches, equipment, everything. In this runaway scrape, as the settlers called it later, they looked to the strongest man and the most courageous they could find for leadership: Sam Houston. In his weatherbeaten slouch hat, creased to three corners like the hat of a patriot of '76, a black cape flopping across his shoulders, he stood out above the mob like a headlight.

But he made hundreds angry because he would not disclose his plans, nor would he fight. It was, "Ride to the east," and that was all. Numbers left him in disgust and returned to try to defend their homes. Many lost confidence in this original character, but he wanted time to raise an army worthy of the name.

Finally he and his men forded the Brazos and camped thirty miles farther east, in an elbow between the San Jacinto * River and a winding stream, Buffalo Bayou.

March rains made the roads quagmires and the streams brim full. At night, campfires chased the gloom in the Texans' camp. Houston made the rounds, telling his men, "We will meet the enemy. To win, some of us may be killed, and *must* be killed."

The men had little to say about this. Instead they told one another stories of the heroes who fell at the Alamo. How Davy Crockett killed so many bears that when he took his rifle, Old Betsy, and climbed a sycamore after one, the bear said, "Don't shoot, Davy, I'll come down." They told how Big Jim Bowie fought a duel on a sandbar in the Mississippi and how, when he was wounded, he drew his Bowie knife and plunged it into one of his enemies, Maj. Norris Wright. "Damn you, Bowie," Wright said, "you've killed me!" They told the tale of Big Jim at a church meeting when he thirsted for knowledge at a time when hecklers made it impossible to listen to the preacher. "I want to hear him read the Good

* In Spanish "Jacinto" is pronounced "Ha-cinto." Texans pronounce it "Ja-cinto," speaking the first syllable softly.

Book," Bowie said. "The next who talks 'll get his windpipe cut."

Houston's men, warming themselves about the campfires, figured out why Bill Travis did not blow up the Alamo and leave it; now on the banks of the San Jacinto they wished he had given them even more time.

"Deaf" Smith and other scouts rode in and reported to Sam Houston that Santa Anna and about twelve-hundred Mexicans were encamped across the prairie eight miles away. Houston ordered Smith and six volunteers to burn Vince's Bridge, stretching across a bayou near the Mexican rear. The two armies were approximately equal. Would Sam Houston never turn and fight?

It was four in the afternoon of April 21, 1836, when Houston and his nine hundred weary men swept across the prairie and attacked. They gained surprise. The Mexicans thought it too late in the day for a fight. The pioneers smashed into them, howling: *"Remember the Alamo!"*

The unready Mexicans tried to run, but they were trapped by a swamp at their backs and by the absence of the bridge. About 630 Mexicans died, Houston losing nine. He was among the wounded—a bullet in his foot.

Santa Anna showed little courage in the pinch. To save his life he took off his general's uniform and donned the rough clothing of a private.

The Battle of San Jacinto, while small, can be listed among the most important ever fought in the Western Hemisphere, because it gave the Texans their freedom.

Sam Houston, now a hero—although not everyone believed he had used the best strategy—was elected the first president of the Texas Republic. Santa Anna, a prisoner and thoroughly frightened, signed that he would never take up arms again against Texas and promised that if he were released the pioneers would be given their freedom. He was imprisoned, then released, President Andrew Jackson using his influence to have him freed. As it turned out, it would have been far better for the United States, Texas, and Mexico had this plotter been kept in prison.

The Mexicans now felt convinced that the Texans were a warlike, belligerent people. Walt Whitman, writing later, saw them differently. In his *Leaves of Grass* he wrote of their boldness and dynamic energy:

> They were the glory of the race of rangers,
> Matchless with horse, rifle, song, supper,
>   courtship,
> Large, turbulent, generous, handsome, proud
>   and affectionate,
> Bearded, sunburnt, drest in the free costume
>   of hunters.

5   BACKGROUND: BOUNDARY WAR AND ANNEXATION

MORE immigrants traveled to Texas. They came across the Gulf in steamers, through the forests of East Texas in covered wagons heaped high with their belongings, or riding horseback from almost every point of the compass, carrying their weapons, with only a blanket and a meal or two tied to the saddles. The success of the Texas Revolution, and hard times in the United States when 618 banks failed, pushed immigrants toward the new republic. Before they left home, many from the Southern states chalked on the doors of their abandoned farms, "GTT"—"Gone to Texas."

This was the year, 1837, that President Jackson, with the approval of Congress, recognized the Republic of Texas.

About 58,000 people now lived in the new country—30,000 Americans, almost 4,000 Mexicans, 5,000 Negro slaves, and 20,000 Indians.

Sam Houston and his countrymen faced enormous problems. Because of the lack of money, taxes could not be collected to support an army or navy, and when currency was issued, the value of the Texas dollar fell to three cents. Another question concerned the Indians who roamed at will. Houston loved the redskins, but President Lamar, who followed him, hated them. He caused ten tribes to be chased out of the country. It was a story of broken promises and unjust treatment.

Lamar encouraged education, but the new country needed more than that.

When France, Holland, and Belgium recognized the new republic, Texas gained in the next three years. To try to move ahead financially, President Lamar sent a force of about three hundred men into New Mexico. His dream was that, if he had soldiers in Santa Fe, trade between that post and northern Mexico would fall into the Texas treasury. This was 1841. Not only did his idea fail, but his soldiers were captured and marched to Mexico in chains. His scheme stirred hatred. Mexicans marched north, raiding the country as far as San Antonio, capturing that town long enough to gather prisoners.

Affairs coasted downhill fast. The Texas government owed seven million dollars. The Indians were in an ugly mood. The country turned to "Old Sam" Houston and elected him president again. In the next six months Great Britain recognized Texas, principally through the efforts of William Kennedy, an Englishman who knew Texas people and conditions. Recognition by Great Britain was splendid, but Texas worried about Mexico. There was certainly no friendly recognition there.

Border warfare seared the countryside. Raiders from south of the Rio Grande placed lonely ranches under attack. Again a Mexican army pushed up as far as San Antonio and captured the town. Texans fought hard and recaptured it.

To retaliate, about three hundred Texans decided to raid Mexico—in spite of Sam Houston's disapproval. They forded the Rio Grande and struck the border town of Mier. One hundred and seventy-six of the Texans were captured, and the treacherous Santa Anna ordered death for one of every ten. To decide who would die, the prisoners were forced to draw beans from a jar. A black bean meant death, a white one meant prison.

In 1842 an American naval officer, miles away from Texas, irritated the Mexicans. A man as odd as his name, Commodore Thomas Ap Catesby Jones steamed into the bay at Monterey, California. Because he had heard a rumor that the United States was at war with Mexico, he captured the Mexican post there. When he learned the truth he apologized, but Mexicans thought they knew what Americans were contemplating.

To the people of Texas, there seemed to be but one solution to trouble with Mexico: annexation by the United States.

Anson Jones, who became the last president of the Republic of Texas, once said, "Texas is like a rich jewel lying derelict by the way." Numbers of Americans realized the wealth that might be obtained there, although they could not foresee such assets as oil.

Cross currents became stronger. Abolitionists of New England feared that Texas would enter the Union as a slave state or as several slave states. This was their great nightmare. Because they hated slavery with a passion, they wanted slaves freed *at once*. Thought of a civil war or wrecking the Union did not concern the abolitionists.

Sam Houston worked as hard as he could for annexation. Nine years back the Texans had voted to enter the Union but the United States had refused. When it appeared that England might get the "jewel," Old Sam shrewdly withdrew the plea for annexation. More and more Texas cotton found its way to England. Suddenly, in the United States, annexation appeared to be a splendid idea. The bitter War of 1812 still inflamed people's minds. It was unthinkable, only thirty-two years later, to allow Texas to become an ally of England.

It seemed right to Americans to annex the Republic of Texas if it wanted to become a state—Texas had been independent for over nine years. The Texans were a kindred people. If Texas were under the Stars and Stripes, more Southerners who wished to move there would be encouraged; also Northerners could sell manufactured products in Texas without paying duty.

On his last day in office, President John Tyler's light-blue eyes riveted on a paper on his desk. Gone was his usual humorous twinkle. Mexico had warned that annexation meant a declaration of war.

John Quincy Adams, former President, respected for his knowledge, thundered that annexation would be the first step in setting up a "slave-tainted" empire. Almost as many Americans were against annexation as were for it.

Henry Thoreau of Concord, Massachusetts, powerful social critic who was also a naturalist—and sometimes an eccentric—protested against the war, and against a government that allowed slavery, by refusing to pay his poll tax. He spent a night in jail and attracted attention to his beliefs. He said that being released made him "as mad as the devil."

Poets and writers in New England worked in their effective way. Later their propaganda, much of it unjust, seeped into history books, picturing the United States as utterly wrong in the years 1845–48.

Just before his term expired, President Tyler signed a joint resolution of Congress inviting Texas to become a state in the Union, and Sam Houston, the man who built Texas into a nation, realized his greatest dream.

Mexicans were furious with the United States. Although the new President, James K. Polk, was almost an unknown, they realized he stood for expansion. He was elected because voters believed that if he were President there was a good chance of acquiring Texas, California, and Oregon.

James Polk's Democratic platform of 1844 was the acme of cleverness. He pretended that the United States had annexed Texas with the Louisiana Purchase in 1803. But if this had been true once, it was certainly *not* true in 1844, because the United States had signed away any rights she might have had twenty-five years earlier in a treaty with Spain. Voters were excited. They shouted, "Reannex Texas!" Over and over, Polk repeated this slogan.

A month after he entered the White House, Congress passed an act offering Texas a place as a state.

On July 4, 1845, in Austin, representatives of the Texans voted unanimously for Texas to enter the Union, and six months later the Congress of the United States approved. But being part of the Union did not end the troubles, because there was no end to violence on the border.

President Polk, a bit prim and severe looking, an intense worker, strong-willed and studious, lived in air castles. This unimaginative man could not put himself in the place of the proud and tenacious Mexicans. In the boundary dispute Mexico was very likely right, because when Texas was part of Mexico the Nueces River was her southern boundary.

Polk sent John Slidell as Minister to Mexico in late 1845, with orders to convince the Mexicans it was best to recognize the Rio Grande as the boundary instead of the Nueces River. He instructed Slidell to tell them that, if they agreed to the new boundary, $2 million worth of claims for damages by Mexican revolutionists to the property of Americans who lived in Mexico would be settled by the United States. Polk also told Slidell to try to buy territory—he could go as high as $25 million for California, for New Mexico $5 million. But the Mexicans refused to talk to him.

The Mexican government, tyrannical and chaotic, had suffered revolution after revolution. In addition, the Mexican people could not understand the grasping people from the north.

Leaders in Mexico City felt sure they could win if it came to war. They knew their cavalry ranked among the best in the world, and they expected it could ride well up into the slave states. The cavalry alone could punish the *gringos*. And, for the large part, the Mexican army was composed of veterans seasoned in the civil wars.

Top Mexican generals knew the United States had no officer who had ever commanded as many as a thousand soldiers.

There was little difference in the population of the two countries. Because war would be fought on Mexican soil, part of the Mexican people would suffer. However, fighting in Mexico was an extreme advantage to Mexican generals because they knew the land, and supply problems would be almost nonexistent when compared to those of the United States.

Mexican politicians were proud. Territorially Mexico was

much larger than the country to the north. Mexico was the fourth largest country in the world—only Russia, Imperial China, and Brazil being larger. The United States was richer, but some Mexican civil leaders believed war would stimulate prosperity—certainly it would bring Texas back under the Mexican flag.

Along the Mexican coast the talk went that Mexican privateers could get rich quickly by raiding American shipping, and leaders in Mexico said, "The *gringos* will run at the first cannon shot. If they don't, yellow fever will eat them up."

In the United States it looked for a while as if there would be *two* wars because of difficulties with Great Britain over rich lands in Oregon and Washington. Many Americans were beginning to say that everything between the Atlantic and the Pacific was theirs—for as far north and south as we could shove the neighbors. Fortunately, the Oregon Treaty of 1846 cleared the situation in the Pacific Northwest. Immigrants began to toil overland and round the Horn to that region.

James Polk did not want war, but he was taking no chances of getting off to a slow start with Mexico. He sent "secret and confidential" orders to Commodore Sloat, US Navy, top officer of a squadron of warships in the Pacific: "The Mexican ports . . . are said to be open and defenceless. . . . [If war comes] occupy San Francisco and other Mexican ports. . . ." War was rushing over the horizon.

Americans felt even more confident than the Mexicans. They considered themselves superior and had been talking down to the Mexicans ever since Stephen Austin brought his settlers to the Brazos River country. They felt sure they would win, although the United States had no war plans and but a tiny army.

When James Polk heard that Mexico refused to talk to John

Slidell, he underestimated the Mexicans. Polk still lived in his air castle. On January 13, 1846, he ordered Taylor to march his handful of soldiers, when he was ready, across the Nueces River to the north bank of the Rio Grande through the disputed territory—with the idea that a show of force would cause the Mexicans to make a deal for peace.

"[But] in case of war," General Taylor's orders read, "your main object will be the protection of Texas."

Old soldier Taylor was narrow and not well-educated. He knew nothing of the more advanced branches of army operations such as fortifications, siege operations, and intelligence. Probably he never realized there was such a thing as strategy. He had confidence in his ability to command men; probably with his background he did this naturally, without much thought. If he saw a driver who could not get his horses to pull a cannon up a hill, he was not above riding close to the man and pulling his ear.

The army laughed over stories about him. Once when he was sitting on a log in his shirt sleeves near his tent, polishing his sword, a new lieutenant rode up. "I say," began the officer. "I've just come, and I want to meet General Taylor. Do you know him?"

Taylor went ahead working on his sword. "Well, I guess I know the old hoss," he said.

"Can't you say 'sir'?" the lieutenant said.

"I guess I can. Yes, sir."

"How about pointing out the general to me?"

"I am General Taylor."

In Mexico with him and other leaders were young men who would win everlasting fame twenty years later in the Civil War: U. S. Grant, R. E. Lee, Thomas Jonathan ("Stonewall") Jackson, William Tecumseh Sherman, George H.

Thomas, Braxton Bragg, P. G. T. Beauregard, George B. McClellan, Jefferson Davis, and a host of others.

During the excitement and confusion of battle, Old Rough and Ready Taylor was unshaken. One historian said, "Everything Taylor did was wrong from a military point of view, except win battles." He was a fearless, determined leader, who would help remake the map of North America and would become President of the United States.

6   TO THE RESCUE AT PALO ALTO
AND RESACA

IMMEDIATELY a problem confronted General Taylor. Scouts rode into the fort his young engineers were building opposite Matamoros, with news that "the enemy in large numbers" was crossing the Rio Grande near his supply base on the Gulf of Point Isabel (now called Port Isabel). He hated to abandon the fort, but a Mexican force could cut off his food and ammunition. What was he to do?

The general scratched his head. Then he had an idea. He would hurry downstream to protect Point Isabel at the mouth of the Rio Grande, and he would leave Maj. Jacob Brown and a small garrison in the fort with some of the cannons. The guns would be under Lt. Braxton Bragg.

It was hot, but the general hiked his men rapidly over the eighteen-mile trail to Point Isabel. He found no enemy, and now came a series of *booms* from back up the river. Obviously Major Brown and his men at the fort were under attack.

Excitement swept the little port of Point Isabel. The soldiers and sailors pictured the enemy as swarming over the walls of the fort—another Alamo. Both wanted to hurry back and attack. Taylor's new dilemma was three-sided: He had a fort eighteen miles away, a valuable supply base on the Gulf of Mexico, and a small force—if he moved, he would have to leave some men to guard Point Isabel.

To learn about conditions in the fort, Taylor called upon a Texas Ranger. The Texas Rangers, a small force organized in the midst of the Texas Revolution, had already proved their value. They were not soldiers but armed police—picked men, un-uniformed, undrilled, sometimes undisciplined, but "unmatched in courage." The man Taylor selected, a former army fighter from Maryland, possessed a top reputation. Ranger Capt. Sam Walker, one of the most popular men on the force, had been on dangerous scouts before and "proved his leadership every day."

He slipped into the night with ten other Rangers—volunteers. A few days later he and his scouts returned from their perilous mission with information for General Taylor: Mexicans in numbers unknown blocked the road to the fort; Major Brown still had ammunition for his cannons, and he was holding out.

Taylor issued the order:

Headquarters, Army of Occupation
May 7, 1846

The army will march at 3 o'clock in the direction of Matamoros. It is known the enemy has recently occupied the route in force. The commanding general has every confidence in his officers and men . . . let the enemy meet him in what numbers they may. He wishes to enjoin upon the battalions of Infantry that their main dependence must be in the bayonet.

This was Taylor's thinking, but his assistant adjutant general, William Bliss, not long ago one of Colonel Thayer's cadets at West Point, wrote it. When Taylor took up a pen, his sentences stretched farther than his advance guard. He was smart to have Major "Perfect" Bliss write most of his orders and reports to Washington.

Taylor did not know the size of the Mexican resistance blocking the road, but he barged ahead. To force the passage, Taylor had 2,281 soldiers and ten cannons. (There were somewhere between three thousand and six thousand Mexican soldiers with twelve pieces of artillery in the 1½-mile-long battle line. The Mexicans say they had three thousand; the Americans estimated them at six thousand.)

A little over halfway to the fort, Taylor found the Mexicans at Palo Alto—"Tall Timber." He stopped his horse near a stream, in no hurry. "Let the men fill their canteens," he said.

Across the dusty plain, General Arista rode the battle lines. He was a political general. When he was placed in command over General Ampudia, the latter resented it. The two Mexican leaders barely spoke to each other.

At three in the afternoon the two armies were a half mile apart. It was an exciting time for the Americans. Would they be overwhelmed? Taylor's three batteries, interspersed between his infantry companies, roared the first shots. Back thundered the Mexican cannons, but most of their fire passed overhead.

Out of the Mexican lines galloped a thousand lancers, heading for Taylor's right wing and for his wagon train. Capt. Sam Ringgold, one of Taylor's efficient artillerymen from West Point, went into action in a new direction. With the help of the 5th and 3rd Infantry Regiments, his battery devastated the lancers.

Battery commanders of the American artillery did not hesitate to move their guns during the battle at Palo Alto. Their fire tore gaps in the Mexican line. A setting sun, ghastly red, filtered through clouds of smoke and dust. Prairie grass caught fire in front of one of Duncan's guns. Tongues of flame cut up into the black smoke. The battlefield became obscured. Lt. George McCall of Pennsylvania wrote: "We tried to extinguish the prairie fire but the red flames began to dance. The smoke drifted along our battle line."

The American battery commanders leaped at the chance to bring up fresh horses and ammunition for the guns, and to have the wounded carried to the rear under cover of the smoke. Captain Ringgold fell, mortally wounded by a round shot.

Now came the determined Mexican infantry in another attack, arcing from their right toward Taylor's center. Captain Duncan's battery hooked up its horses and dashed forward to help the 8th Infantry Regiment. Cannister and grapeshot mowed the Mexicans down. They left the field, retreating in disarray into the night, carrying about three hundred wounded with them. Behind lay two hundred of their dead.

General Taylor spurred his horse forward to make sure the infantry sent out patrols, then he rode back to an improvised hospital where his surgeons worked. He felt like his soldiers—almost intoxicated by the victory. It had cost fifty-six in killed and wounded, but the Mexican army had been defeated. The skill of the American artillery amazed Old Rough and Ready Taylor. Never again would he doubt what his fast-moving horse-drawn artillery and the redleg gunners could do.

The noise of the fight at Palo Alto drifted back to Point Isabel, and when a shocked camp follower staggered in with a story about "Taylor's defeat," the navy worried. Young sailors formed to go to the rescue of the army, but Commodore David Conner wisely stopped them.

Taylor still did not know if the road to Fort Texas lay open, and to find out he pushed scouts forward at daylight. They soon returned with word that the Mexicans held a new position—blocking the road four miles from the fort, at the Resaca de la Palma. The horseshoe-shaped ravine, waist-deep in mud and water, formed a cavity fifty yards wide. Chaparral—thickets of dwarf evergreen oaks and thorny shrubs—

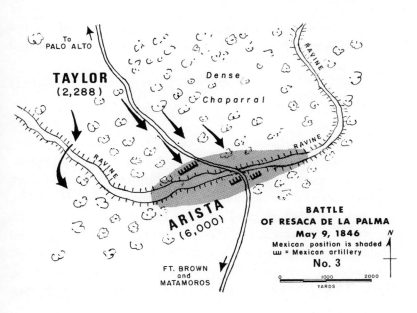

TAYLOR
(2,288)

TO PALO ALTO

Dense Chaparral

RAVINE

ARISTA
(6,000)

FT. BROWN
and
MATAMOROS

**BATTLE
OF RESACA DE LA PALMA
May 9, 1846**
Mexican position is shaded
ɯ = Mexican artillery

No. 3

0   1000   2000
YARDS

helped to conceal the position. General Arista's artillery could sweep the approaches, and he had both sides of the ravine lined with his infantrymen. The place looked like a death trap.

Here the Mexican artillerymen had the advantage; chaparral blocked the American artillery from getting into position where it could fire. The Mexicans felt confident; at one end of the line Mexican bands played a concert.

1st Lt. George McCall scouted ahead on a horse. Behind him came a hundred infantrymen and a handful of dragoons. The chaparral was thick. He worried about ambush; at this time there was no positive information about the enemy. He wrote after the battle:

> I got within 250 yards of the ravine and saw 3 *rancheros* (irregular Mexican cavalrymen). They saw us but did nothing. [Soon] I became satisfied that the enemy was there in strength, and I sent three dragoons to inform General Twiggs. I took up a position within 150 yards of the Mexicans. I was much obliged that General Arista decided to await our attack. . . .
> In a short time I rode to find the headquarters and staff. General Twiggs said to me, "Well, what have we here?"
> "The Mexicans in full dress uniform, sir," I said.
> "Is there a position for our artillery?" he said.
> "There is, General. I will show them where to unlimber."

The dense chaparral worried the American gunners. Taylor sent his infantry forward. Units became intermingled in the matted growth. It was like night fighting. Officers found themselves commanding men they had never seen before. On top of it all, Mexican artillerymen dashed from the concert, manned their cannons, and blasted canister through the woods. General Taylor sent for Capt. Charles May.

Later, some charged that Taylor never gave orders in a battle. This was false. Now he snapped at May, "I want your dragoons to charge down this road and knock out that battery."

It looked like suicide. To reach the seven-gun battery, the dragoons trotted ahead along the road, hugging the chaparral as long as they could. Then they spurred their mounts. The dash along the road sounded like an approaching windstorm. Bending low over the necks of their running horses, the Americans charged into the battery. Some aimed pistols alongside the necks of their horses. Others had sabers thrust forward like spears.

The Mexicans fired. Seven dragoons and eighteen horses crashed into a bloody heap. Some of the Mexicans, surprised, fled into the chaparral. Near a cannon the dragoons found General Vega. They took him prisoner and grabbed his sword. The Mexican artillerymen scrambled back courageously to fight with swords, pistols, and rifles.

When Lt. Randolph Ridgely, battery commander, saw the dragoons go in, on his own he brought his battery forward down the road at a gallop. It unlimbered quickly and went into action. The battery roared. The range was twenty-five yards.

Taylor sent back in a hurry for his wagon train guards, the 8th Infantry Regiment. They came forward at double time and pitched in. The 5th Infantry Regiment worked its way through the chaparral and joined the hand-to-hand fighting. The surprise blow of the dragoons, artillery, and infantry at the center of the line was too much for the Mexicans. They broke and tore for the river.

Weary soldiers in nearby Fort Texas sped them on their way by firing the last of their shells. The soldiers in the fort had held out for about 108 hours of enemy attack, and part of this time they had been bombarded with red-hot cannonballs.

Their morale was high although their commander, Maj. Jacob Brown, lay dead. A cannonball had smashed his leg. He died from that and from the shock of the amputation operation. Taylor ordered the fort renamed Fort Brown in his honor, and later the town nearby became Brownsville.

When exchange of prisoners occurred, Captains Thornton and Hardee and others returned to the American camp. Vega was in no hurry to go back to Mexico. It was no place for a defeated general.

The American leader sounded like a knight when he shook Vega by the hand, saying, "General, I assure you I deeply regret that this misfortune has fallen upon you. I regret it sincerely, and I take great pleasure in returning this sword which you have worn with so much gallantry." Vega made a flowery reply and then became the guest of Old Davy the Bengal Tiger.

Taylor followed the defeated Mexicans about sixty miles, then turned back to Fort Brown to wait for supplies and reinforcements.

The victory at Resaca cost 39 American lives and 71 in wounded. The Americans captured 8 cannons, 2,000 rifles and muskets, 200 mules, and stacks of ammunition and supplies, as well as General Arista's public correspondence. The Mexicans lost over 800 in killed and wounded.

In 1846 communications moved almost at an ant's pace. In Washington on May 9 President Polk received Taylor's message of April 26 about the clash on the Rio Grande, when the Mexicans overpowered Thornton and his sixty-eight dragoons. Polk assembled his cabinet.

At noon on May 12 the President, looking more severe than ever, white hair hanging behind his ears and framing his thin face, said, ". . . war . . . notwithstanding all our efforts to avoid it, exists by act of Mexico herself." He recommended a declaration of war.

Sen. John C. Calhoun, South Carolinian, old War Hawk of 1812, who as Secretary of State for Tyler had helped bring Texas into the Union, led the objectors. There was a stormy debate. Calhoun pleaded for a pause. Few legislators wanted to wait. The House voted for war, 174–14; the Senate, 40–2. On May 13, 1846, Polk signed the bill and the country went to war.

War fever raged more mildly in New England than in other parts of the country. In New York signs appeared: MEXICO OR DEATH!

Volunteers fumed. They wanted to join Old Rough and Ready immediately. In New Orleans, Gen. Edmund P. Gaines, the "Recruiting Genius," was on fire to secure volunteers for Taylor.

Gaines, sixty-nine years old, fixed it in his head that it was his duty to plunge into a recruiting campaign. He worked feverishly to ship raw recruits to Taylor. Gaines appointed officers on his own, enlisting all kinds of specialists: chaplains, clerks, adjutants, quartermasters, blacksmiths, and so on with little rhyme or reason.

The war was young but people knew of the first hero: Old Rough and Ready Taylor. Newspapers wrote of him at Resaca sitting on Old Whitey, sword drawn, while musket balls hummed. However, a few thinking army officers wondered about his strategy, or lack of it.

President Polk had gambled by sending such a small army to the disputed territory, but so far he and Taylor had won. However, the President was not sure about Taylor's generalship—ability to plan and direct campaigns. When Polk heard how Taylor had moved up and down the river from his supply base, building a fort, then leaving it—he worried.

A new trouble plagued Polk when "war" broke out in Washington between the Recruiting Genius and General Scott, the Army's top leader. Scott wrote a 150-page pamphlet castigating Gaines and had it published. Scott said that Gaines was "an antique, fit only to be a nurse in a lying-in hospital," and that Gaines's trouble came from "being insane or from being in his dotage."

The Recruiting Genius declared that if he had fifty battalions of mounted gunmen, plus the army in Texas, he could terminate the war in six months. As to his age, he snorted, "I am three years younger than Field Marshal Blucher was in his last brilliant actions near Waterloo.... I claim the right to command.... Scott has been working against me for over a quarter of a century to defeat my efforts."

To Polk, it seemed his senior warriors were as anxious to fight each other as the Mexicans. In this paper war, Polk backed Winfield Scott, and Gaines received orders to come to Washington for trial.

The Baltimore *Patriot* reacted by defending Gaines: "Shame on the Administration! ... General Gaines acted according to the emergency!" Gaines proved a good lawyer, although cruel phrases against Winfield Scott rolled from his tongue.

The court-martial found Gaines guilty of calling out volunteers illegally and of violating orders, but let him off easily. Finally an order sent him to New England, where he spent the war.

Next came the argument over brevet rank between General Haughty Bill Worth and General Twiggs. Fortunately Worth, sorry that he had missed Palo Alto and Resaca, started back to join General Taylor.

Old Rough and Ready Taylor was not easy for everyone to serve under. He disliked volunteers and many of the young West Point officers who were "raised by the book." He had little charity and much venom in his personality, and as the war progressed, he grew more and more irritable. Narrowness and illiteracy are exposed in his letters. Perfect Bliss could have been well employed as private secretary to the old general as well as assistant adjutant general. Taylor wrote about Worth to his son-in-law, Dr. R. C. Wood, army surgeon at Point Isabel:

[Worth acts modestly] but the fact is between ourselves, he has been pampered and bloated for things he never done, or acts he never performed, but from assumption, & getting others to state occurrencies the truth of which may be very well called in question, if stronger language could not be properly applied, and his flourish among the wounded was in keeping with many other of his acts, all for effect. . . .

But as jealous as Taylor was of Worth, he needed him. The former West Point commandant had proved his dash on the Niagara frontier in the War of 1812. At Lundy's Lane, almost every American officer was killed or wounded. Worth had a leg wound, but this did not stop him. And later against the Winnebagos in Wisconsin Territory and against the Seminoles, he proved he was still a leader. So determined was his drive in the Everglades—in the heat of a Florida summer— some of his contemporaries said, "Haughty Bill Worth is crazy." Others admired him and called him the Murat of the American Army, after the marshal of Napoleon.

Worth's bronzed, weather-beaten face gave him the look of a hero. Worth liked to say, "My headquarters are in the saddle, sir." This statement sums him up. The historian Edward S. Wallace compared his extraordinary magnetism and his warm personality with that of a dashing American general who fought a century later, George S. Patton. Wallace also wrote, "Worth probably realized more fully than did Taylor the bloody fighting which lay ahead."

While General Taylor waited after the battle of Resaca, spies and scouts brought him word that the Mexicans were reorganizing the army and were strengthening the defenses of Monterrey, a fortified city guarding a pass in the mountains 170 hard miles from Matamoros.*

As long as the two countries were at war, a Mexican force in Monterrey posed a threat to the Rio Grande country.

* See Map. No. 4, page 57.

7   GENERALS ASSORTED

Back in Washington, the hard-working President had his trouble moving the war ahead. He felt shaky about Zachary Taylor. The question was: Could he lead an army—could he make the thousands of decisions an army commander had to make?

Winfield Scott knew the answer. Later he wrote in his *Memoirs* of Zachary Taylor's virtues: "... great character, uncorrupted morals, indomitable courage." Then Scott gave the background that limited Taylor: "Frontier and small military posts had been his home. He was quite ignorant for his rank and bigoted in his ignorance." In discussing his education, Scott said that Taylor knew nothing of literature "much beyond good old Dilworth's Spelling Book."

The President considered Winfield Scott himself for the command, but he felt uneasy because the famous general was a Whig. Politics guided Polk as if he were a sea captain and political leadership a compass. He looked upon Scott as an opponent—presidential timber—who might become the next President. Polk wanted to save the Presidency for himself, or at least for another Democrat.

Today we know more of Polk and his thoughts than of most of his contemporaries, because he kept a diary—published in 1910. On May 13, 1846, he wrote:

I tendered to Gen'l Scott the command of the army to be raised. He accepted.... Though I did not consider him in all respects suited ... yet being commander-in-chief, his position entitled him to it. Most of the Cabinet were in attendance....

People knew about Scott's leadership at Fort George on the Niagara River and at the Battle of the Chippewa. He emerged from the War of 1812 as *the* hero. At Fort George he was sensational. There he galloped his horse into the hard-pressed fort, with two companies of infantrymen, to save the powder magazine from exploding. But before they could extinguish the burning fuses, it blew up. A stone, descending from the explosion, smashed his left collarbone. He fell from his mount, seized an ax, and with his good arm chopped down the flagpole to grab the British flag.

In 1812, on a cholera-ridden ship crossing Lake Erie, his soldiers said, "Scott commanded the cholera to stop—and it did."

He was a giant and looked it. Over six feet four at two hundred pounds, his eating habits had not yet burdened him with the extra flesh that handicapped him later, at the start of the Civil War. Now, in 1846, Scott was sixty, but as virile as a man of forty.

When he mounted his horse at a review, a crusader-size sword hanging from his belt, his plumed hat made him appear taller than he was. In the ceremony, when the time came for him to inspect the soldiers, he galloped down the line, his hat in one hand as a mark of respect, his reins in the other. Scott was spectacular.

In honor of the fight of his brigade at the battle at Chippewa in the War of 1812, the cadets at West Point received the order to wear gray cloth—the color of the uniforms of Scott's soldiers.

General Scott liked West Point and its cadets. He went there when he could, and sometimes, to the surprise of an instructor, he took over a class. The cadets enjoyed him. They said he was inspecting them so he might select a future aide. People relished stories on Scott—about his bravery, his vanity, and his eating. The general was proud of his size. Once in a western tavern a stranger mistook him for a bartender and ordered a drink. The old general fixed the stranger with his blue eyes and thundered, "Did you ever know anyone six feet, four and a quarter inches tall to sell rum, sir?"

Earl Schenk Miers, writing over a hundred years later about Scott, said, "He never forsook the loves of his youth—canvasback duck, claret, the army, the Constitution, and the Union." Scott liked to get off the conversation stopper: "I was three years old when the Constitution was adopted."

A governor of Virginia characterized him: "What a wonderful mixture . . . ostentation, fuss, feathers, bluster, and genuine soldierly talent and courage is Winfield Scott!"

Not everyone appreciated him. A strong man, a giant in the story of the United States Army, he made strong enemies.

Some officers jeered behind his back, giving him his nickname, "Old Fuss and Feathers"; but in this war he became one of the greatest military leaders of American history.

A three-way muddle developed in Washington in late May, 1846. Scott's boss, Secretary of War William Marcy, a shrewd executive, understood politics but knew little about an army or about running a war. He thought Scott belonged at the front. So did the President. Trouble started when Mr. Marcy discovered that the general had decided to remain in Washington and to direct the war from there rather than travel to the Rio Grande. This upset both politicians.

An interchange of letters started, and Scott was at a disadvantage. He used blundering, unpolished phrases; he wrote Marcy that if he had an adequate army he could land on the Mexican Gulf at Vera Cruz, march to Mexico City, and "conquer a peace."

If anyone *could* "conquer a peace," it was probably Winfield Scott.

His private note found its way into the papers, and this hurt, but it did not stop him. Angrily he wrote Marcy that he was working fifteen to eighteen hours a day, and that "I am too old a soldier and have too much *special* experience not to feel the importance of securing my rear of ill-will and condemnation before advancing against the enemy. . . ."

At the end of this long letter, to be sure that he made his point, Scott finished (you could almost feel his anger), "I do not desire to place myself in the most perilous of all positions: *—a fire upon my rear, from Washington, and the fire in front from the Mexicans.*" For emphasis, he used italics to underscore his slur.

The President, also working long hours, felt incensed. He

was jealous and suspicious of Scott's popularity. Suppose Scott ran for President at the next election?

Marcy replied for the Administration, writing Scott that his letter reflected on the President and asking how he could possibly make such charges. Marcy went on to say that President Polk had decided to swallow the insult and directed Scott to prepare for vigorous prosecution of the war.

This correspondence also found its way to the papers, and people howled over Scott's reply: "Your letter came at about 6:00 P.M., as I sat down to take a hasty plate of soup. . . ." The idea of the famous trencherman, who sometimes told hostesses how and what to cook, and who could roast a ham as well as any chef, settling for "a hasty plate of soup," amused people.

Scott's reply rambled. He praised the President for not putting him in arrest and before a court-martial, then he backtracked and charged in all directions like Don Quixote. Scott said—among other things—in a 167-word sentence, that he knew friends of the President condemned him because "I did not fly to the Rio Grande, without waiting for the invading army to be raised. . . ." He closed, "Whether it shall be the pleasure of the President to send me to the Rio Grande (which I would prefer) or to retain me here, I can only say I am [anxious] to do my duty."

The letters, published in the press, almost destroyed Scott's usefulness. Reporters harpooned him, but now he kept quiet and worked at the task of forming an army.

For a while the President and the Secretary labored harmoniously with the general, although Scott bored them with endless details of logistics. He showed columns of figures on supplies needed: the number of cannon, shells, bullets, rifles, muskets, pistols, swords, bayonets, wagons, oxen, mules, horses, saddles, bridles, horseshoes; the amount of black powder, uniforms, shoes, rations, etc.

Both Polk and Scott burned with anxiety to get the job done but each in his own way. The President and his advisors pored over the sketchy maps of Mexico.

Scott, magnificent in his blue-and-gold uniform, dwarfed the frail James K. Polk. The President and his Cabinet listened to Scott because of the general's vast experience. He talked about landing on the Gulf at Vera Cruz and pushing inland, but the President, with the approval of Scott, decided to set several drives in motion. The principal operation in 1846 was given to Old Rough and Ready against Monterrey.

Orders went to the Navy to blockade ports in the Gulf of Mexico.

Messengers rushed requisitions to the governors of southern states (because they were closer to the scene of the war) for 25,000 men—needed in a hurry. The schedule called for the rest of the country to provide forty thousand.

Because most of the President's advisors thought the war would be short, the soldiers would be enlisted for only twelve months. The militia and volunteers enlisted by Gaines would be expected to serve only six months. To confuse the picture even more, volunteers requested by Taylor from the governors of Texas and Louisiana could go home in three months.

Life was even more chaotic in Mexico. Revolution had torn up the government. José Ramírez, Mexican political expert, wrote: "Public affairs are becoming truly incomprehensible." Who could pull the Mexican people through and lead them against the invaders?

Unfortunately President Polk had been tricked into furnishing the answer. Before the two countries clashed, he fell into a trap. The Mexicans had a leader in exile in Cuba—the cruel

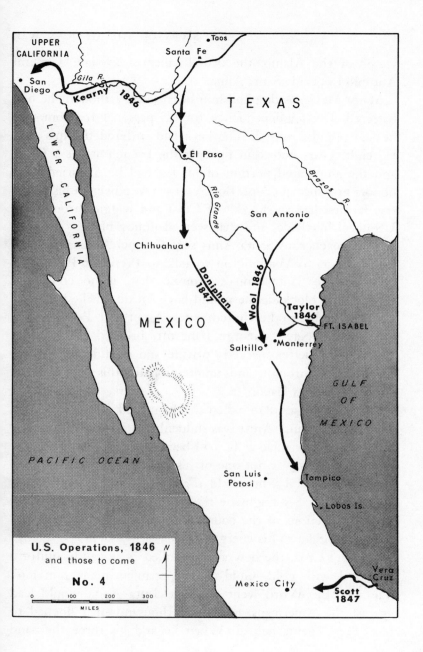

UPPER
CALIFORNIA

San
Diego

Gila R.

Kearny 1846

LOWER CALIFORNIA

Taos

Santa Fe

T E X A S

El Paso

Rio Grande

Brazos R.

San Antonio

Chihuahua

M E X I C O

Doniphan 1847

Wool 1846

Taylor 1846

FT. ISABEL

Saltillo • Monterrey

GULF
OF
MEXICO

PACIFIC OCEAN

San Luis
Potosi

Tampico

Lobos Is.

U.S. Operations, 1846 N
and those to come

No. 4

0   100   200   300
MILES

Mexico City

Vera
Cruz

Scott
1847

victor of the Alamo, the brutal killer of Goliad: General
Antonio López de Santa Anna.

Many Mexicans despised him because they thought he had
bartered Texas independence for his personal freedom, but
he had popular appeal. The hero had suffered the loss of a
leg eight years before in fighting the French at Vera Cruz,
and the amputated portion of his leg had been buried with
honors in a special crypt. But to return to power in his country, he first had to slip out of Cuba and wiggle through the
US naval blockade, and that seemed impossible.

The treacherous Santa Anna sent Colonel Atocha, a Mexican banker, to Washington to talk to President Polk. The
colonel gave Santa Anna's promise that, if he could get
through the blockade, he would have Mexico make peace on
terms favorable to the United States. As a result, Polk's Secretary of the Navy, George Bancroft, ordered Commodore
Conner, in a letter marked "private and confidential" to let
Santa Anna through, and unintentionally this supplied the
Mexicans with a leader.

In mid-August, 1846, when this happened, not every Mexican thought Santa Anna was suddenly an angel. Many knew
he could be a maniac as he had been at the Alamo, and that
trustworthiness was not one of his virtues. But the Mexicans
wanted a general who could throw the *gringos* out, and it
appeared that SA might be the man. They hoped he could
weld the factions of the country. The loss of a leg was certainly no brake to his energy.

In Vera Cruz, the new arrival pulled on a gaudy uniform
plastered with gold. Gold-fringed epaulets made him look
like a husky. Word went out that Santa Anna would lead
against the Americans, and three thousand men flocked to
him. Press agents helped. When he and his three thousand

arrived in Mexico City, he published a proclamation saying he was ready to offer his body to American bullets. "I'm just a soldier fighting for my country," he said. "We can tear the star of Texas from the American flag."

Fortunately for United States soldiers, this power-drunk Mexican general was not as smart as many of his countrymen believed. Thousands of his countrymen misjudged him. Ramírez wrote: "There is no doubt that SA is returning a real democrat."

He returned to find political affairs in Mexico boiling. At a meeting of the Federalist Society, a political club in Mexico City, a leader jumped on the stage, waved a dagger, and said the best way out of the turmoil was to behead the leader of the opposition, Don Lucas Alamán; either that, or "have a Sicilian massacre."

Civil war had broken out in late 1845 among the Carmelites. Some of the friars fought in the cause of religion; others fought because they believed a revolution could cure poverty. About two months before Santa Anna returned from exile, another revolution blazed in west-central Mexico, in the town of Guadalajara. The crisis was made to order for a savior or a knave.

The war did not wait for the Mexican government. Zachary Taylor and his six thousand soldiers began to march on Monterrey.

8   SCOUTS OUT!

Iⁿ his tent in camp on the road to Monterrey, Gen. Zachary Taylor unfolded his tiny field desk and scribbled a letter in his rare style to his son-in-law:

Camp...75 miles from Monterey
September, 10th, 1846

My dear Doctor,

Your very acceptable & interesting letter of the 1st inst reached me on the evening of the 5th the day before we left Comargo for this place, where I arrived yesterday & joined the advance under Genl Worth, finding all well...tow Rgts of Texas mounted men are or have been ordered on a road running parallel to the one we are on to our left, under Govr Henderson to unite with us some fifty miles in advance of this place, should they not disband, of

which there is some apprehension when we left Comargo....
[We are] not far short of 6,000 about 3,200 of which will be
regulars. Whether the enemy will fight for Monterey is quite un-
certain, it can only be ascertained by going there; my impressions
are we shall meet with no resistance out of the city, they may
attempt to defend it, which I hope will be the case, as they have
thrown up some slight defences for its protection; as I hope to be
able to reduce it, in which case I hope to capture their army....
We shall however see all about it when we get there—

There is no doubt but what Santa Anna has returned to
Mexico....

Taylor wrote that near his tent water poured from several
springs that "could supply the city of New York." Brooks of
cool water bubbled alongside the road. To the west a block
of mountains rose four thousand feet. Just before sundown,
purple shadows cut fascinating planes on the slopes, but not
everyone thought the shadows beautiful, because a Mexican
force lying in ambush in the foothills could sweep down and
strike the Americans in the flank. However, Taylor himself
felt assured; the Texas Rangers scouted the foothills and sent
him word: "No signs of enemy."

In the far distance, blocking the line of march, the Sierra
Madre speared upward five thousand feet, a faint blue wall.
Spies, scouts, and Mexican mule drivers said that in front of
the mountains, in the forest surrounding Monterrey, the Mexican Army waited.

Before Taylor marched his army south, it had experienced
hell in the flat land along the Rio Grande. For two months the
sun had tortured the general and his soldiers while they waited,
principally for wagons and steamboats. Why didn't Washington rush transportation?

One reason was the slowness of the mail—by the time Taylor's letters reached Washington almost a month had crept by.

Then, too, neither the War Department nor the country was prepared to equip an army. Delay followed delay.

When steamboats finally arrived to transport soldiers, food, and ammunition upstream from Matamoros to Camargo,* many of the boats drew too much water and others lacked power to overcome the current. Old Rough and Ready's temper grew shorter.

Camargo, Mexico, was literally a jumping-off place for the interior. It sprawled along the river, a flock of dilapidated buildings hovering about a beautiful cathedral. To get there from Matamoros you traveled 127 miles over a dusty road, or if you journeyed by steamboat you went three times that distance. One soldier on a boat said, "The Rio Grande out-crooks the crookedest."

While Taylor waited at Camargo for supplies, sickness attacked his army. Tragedy struck; approximately fifteen hundred soldiers died of disease. Newly arrived volunteers suffered the most. At night mosquitoes "as big as pigeons" feasted on the soldiers, and the insects seemed to prefer the newcomers. The funerals seemed endless. Bands wore themselves out parading to the graveyards along the river, playing the "Dead March." Zach Taylor wrote to Washington for more medicines and more doctors. Word came back that he had *enough* doctors.

To take the minds of the soldiers off their plight and to ready them, Haughty Bill Worth and Davy the Bengal Tiger ordered innumerable drills. The volunteers especially needed practice. General Taylor, content to let Worth and Twiggs train the army, wrote: "I seldom leave my tent."

By early September, 1846, Taylor could stand no more of

* See Map No. 1, page 8.

Camargo. Scouts and Rangers rode in with news that General Ampudia was working feverishly to strengthen the forts around Monterrey, that every day more Mexicans rode into the city and joined his army. Ampudia's lancers were described as especially good.

Taylor saw that the enemy was getting stronger while he was getting weaker. He lost hope of using all of his volunteers. Most of them remained half-acclimated, half-trained. He decided to leave almost ten thousand volunteers behind with doctors to care for the sick and to strike for Monterrey.

The volunteers left behind felt keenly disappointed. They believed that they had paid the price, by their suffering and hours at drill in the sun, to fight Mexicans, but Taylor refused to be weighed down with men he would have to worry about.

One volunteer regiment he did *not* leave behind was the First Texas Rifles—many of them Indian fighters—led by Col. Albert Sidney Johnston. This massively built soldier looked like a prime fullback or a champion boxer in training. Eight years before he had enlisted in the Texas Army; now he was serving in high rank without pay. Taylor adored him. "He's the best soldier I ever commanded," he said.

Not every officer in the influx of volunteers who joined Taylor at Matamoros was a successful leader. Gen. Gideon J. Pillow of Tennessee was a man of unlimited personal courage —energetic, intelligent, but inexperienced. He was a general because he had been a law partner of Polk's and because he had helped to elect him President. Pillow, tall, with quick, deep-set eyes and a short goatee, was anxious to help. However, Taylor felt unsure about him.

One of the Democrats along as second in command to

General Taylor was Maj. Gen. William Butler of Carrollton, Kentucky, who had interrupted a lawyer's career to fight again. Back in 1812, near Detroit, the British had captured Butler, and after being exchanged his bravery stood out when he fought under Old Hickory Jackson at New Orleans.

A volunteer Old Rough and Ready welcomed especially was John Quitman of Mississippi. Years before, Quitman, traveling from New York, had come ashore from a flatboat at Natchez. He followed the Texans' troubles for a long time, once leading a company of Mississippians—the Fencibles—to Texas. Like Butler, Quitman was a lawyer. Quitman was smart, adventurous, popular, and inspirational. On his epaulets he wore the single star of a brigadier general.

Before Taylor marched away from the Camargo pesthole, he held a grand review. Captain Henry wrote: "It was a magnificent display." Not only did Taylor see that his six-thousand-man army was ready, but the soldiers saw their general "in good health or spirits in plain undress uniform."

Taylor regretted he could not take all of his artillery, because of a shortage of horses.

In barging into Mexico the United States was taking on a large order. In the Mexican Army there were 32,000 men. To make matters even more chancy, no American knew for sure where the enemy's army lay.

Out in front of Taylor's soldiers, three days ahead, marched his "pioneers," engineer soldiers who could repair a road, construct a bridge, lay out a fort, and fight. Near them as guards trotted a detachment from Taylor's five hundred dragoons. On the flanks rode Texas Rangers under Capt. Ben McCulloch, part of the regiment of Rangers commanded by Col. John Hays.

The Texas Rangers were even more nonregulation than Zach Taylor. They dressed in red or blue shirts—some in fringed buckskin jackets. Slouch hats were popular, although a number wore straw sombreros tied with buckskin thongs beneath their chins. Their armament varied. Some cradled muskets as they trotted along on wiry mustangs; others boasted of rifles riding snugly in saddle boots. Lassos and small sacks of parched corn dangled from their saddles. Almost every belt supported a Bowie knife and a repeating Colt revolver.

One of the characteristics of the Rangers that helped the army was that they were not roadbound. Where antelopes could go, so could they. Some called the Rangers the Cossacks of the Army, because they did not mind "borrowing" when they rode by a watermelon patch or a cornfield.

Their leader, Col. "Jack" Coffey Hays, had a wiry build, jet black hair, and the features of a Greek statue—but sunburned. His favorite mount was a dark bay war-horse. He was an Indian fighter who had "chased the Comanches to the Rocky Mountains." His bravery had won a commendation from Sam Houston. However, a Lipan Indian characterized Hays by saying, "Capitan Hays great chief, but American eat too much on warpath."

His salty-looking right-hand man, Capt. Ben McCulloch, was also handsome, but when on business he wore a bushy brown moustache and beard that made his mouth seem like the entrance to a cave. Long hair and sideburns framed his face. Ben McCulloch was one of the most popular men in Texas, a friend of Davy Crockett, successful bear hunter, veteran of San Jacinto, and a leader who "helped clean up the Texas Indian trouble." He was fearless. This and his knowledge of

Spanish let him slip into the Mexican lines and come out in one piece.

On a scout before the army marched south into Mexico, McCulloch jumped Antonio Canales, the Chaparral Fox. This border ruffian called himself a general, but he was not above robbing his own people. His spies lurked beyond the fires of American camps, and when they trapped a soldier he was lassoed and shot. McCulloch did not catch the Chaparral Fox, but on the chase McCulloch discovered valuable information about the road to Monterrey, and reported it to General Taylor.

On the march south, far behind the Rangers and the advance guard, the pack train plodded between the rear guard and the wagon train. Taylor's quartermasters had spent large sums for seventeen hundred mules. Special frontiersmen had been recruited to herd and load them. These were the packers. Some of them were Mexican mule drivers, in the pay of the army.

The packers, though sometimes laughed at by the rest of the soldiers, had their own brand of pride. Not everyone could be a packer. Life was hard for them. Sometimes on the march they got up at three in the morning to load the mules. It took training to throw the diamond hitch—lashing bundles wrapped in canvas or in grass mats in a special way to the backs of the animals. Some mules could carry three hundred pounds, others only 120. The packers knew the mules. If you tied a sloppy diamond hitch, even if the mule bucked only a little when the train moved out, supplies tumbled all along the road. Seventeen hundred mules sounds like a huge herd, but Winfield Scott wanted Taylor to take three thousand.

Because he had a limited pack train and not as many wagons as he wanted, Taylor had only enough food for eight days. In war you have to take chances to win, but in striking inland 140 miles this general was gambling on a fast victory. There was ammunition supply to worry about, too. If he failed to overcome the fortified city quickly, his men faced starvation or retreating.

At first the soldiers felt as if they made no headway toward the mountain range in the distance. They hiked fifteen to twenty miles a day and seemed to get nowhere. If they marched over twenty miles the men became unhappy. After the first mile, carrying a pack, a rifle, and forty rounds of ammunition became hard work. Officers in the grades of captain and up rode horses, and they trotted up and down the column talking with one another and checking on the privates.

Although chaparral and sagebrush dotted the countryside, the land gradually lost its semitropical look. The chestnut-colored earth sloped gently upward. Oak, walnut, cypress, and willows appeared, and here and there a pine or a spruce. Yet the sun blistered the soldiers. Many volunteers tossed aside their tin canteens, because "the sun made the water warm and unpleasant." Mexican gourds that kept water cool were more popular. At night, a cold wind made a blanket and an oak fire welcome.

By mid-September the lovely valleys in the mountains stood out. Clouds curled around the jagged peaks. The Sierra Madre Oriental resembled stage scenery or fairy land. Ice plant crowned with tiny pink flowers lined the road. The soldiers marched through villages where "nearly every yard has a great quantity of grapes, pomegranates, and oranges."

The wonderful villagers were friendly. They gave or sold

delicious *tortillas*, thin pancakes of corn; *enchiladas*, with ground chicken, beef, or vegetables rolled up inside; and tasty *frijoles*, beans. The march was a picnic—until enemy cavalry appeared.

9 THE BATTLE OF MONTERREY

THE Mexican cavalry galloped toward Monterrey, red pennants fluttering. Not a shot had been fired. The Mexican horsemen only scattered paper along the road. American infantry, swinging along in their light-blue uniforms, broke the rhythm of their march to pick up the papers. They chuckled at the statement: "PROCLAMATION! WE ARE WAITING WITH OUTSTRETCHED ARMS FOR YOU. *If you join us you will receive land and rewards according to rank.*" United States 1st Lt. Benjamin Alvord wrote: "The Mexicans are preparing for war with the knife. They may be cunning enough to wait, and wait, and wait."

American privates ridiculed the paper, but the officers kept still. Somewhere to the front the deserter Riley, expert gunner who had once taught artillery to the West Point cadets, manned a cannon. It was easy to guess that he would teach artillery to the Mexicans. Back at Matamoros, Sergeant Riley had asked for a pass to attend Mass and failed to return. Enough men had deserted along the Rio Grande and had crossed to the enemy to form a battalion.

In front of the advancing Americans, just out of range, walked several hundred Mexican soldiers. "With them," General Taylor wrote, "are about 50 spies."

He ordered his army into camp twelve miles from Monterrey. The next day's march made the soldiers feel the closeness of the mountains. Taylor trotted forward with his expert topographical engineers—young officers trained in reconnaissance and map making—and a party of Texas Rangers.

With General Taylor rode Lt. George Gordon Meade, eleven years out of West Point. At the head of the army, the general and the lieutenant resembled heroes from the Old Testament looking for gladiators from the opposing army. Meade wrote in a few days to his wife:

We advanced within a mile of their works but could see no sign of their occupation and began to believe they had deserted. Some of our bold fellows pushed nearer. . . . The enemy opened their batteries on us, and fired several times without doing any injury, though one ball passed about two feet on one side of my knee. . . . [Another cannonball whizzed close to Taylor.] Finding we were in range, the General withdrew the Texans and selected a camp some two and a half miles from the town.

Monterrey, eight thousand people, lay cupped in the mountains. Behind it ran a river with two names, the San Juan de Monterrey or the Santa Clara.

In front of the city, barring the way, frowned the Black Fort. From its ramparts floated the green, red, and white flag of Mexico. Monterrey looked tranquil in the afternoon light as if the fort and the gray-green mountains behind the city were protection enough.

The topographical engineers scouted other routes to gain more information. Maj. Joe Mansfield led the way. With him rode Captains Gillespie and William G. Williams and Lieutenant Meade, who sketched a map. The party returned safely, but Williams, who went out again, was shot dead.

By candlelight in Taylor's tent early on Sunday morning, September 20, 1846, the general and his senior officers listened to the reports of the engineers and studied Meade's map. The young officers warned, "Every house is a fort."

Later Taylor wrote:

[They said] the twown [sic] was completely fortified, supplied with a large amount of artillery ... and the streets barracaded, the Houses with very thick walls, with loop holes for small arms, as well as other defenses, & the streets raked by artillery. . . ."

On the 140-mile march many Americans wondered why General Ampudia and his soldiers, about ten thousand, had not slashed out and attacked Taylor's six thousand and his supply train. Now the Mexican defenses looked formidable. Maybe the Mexicans did not need to attack.

The pick of the American army waited General Taylor's word. If he wanted them to smash head first into the Black Fort they were willing to try.

He asked for the opinions of the senior officers, paying particular attention to Haughty Bill Worth, his best soldier. This was no moment for jealousy. In the yellow candlelight Worth's intelligent, chubby face looked older than his fifty-two years. He thought it foolish to storm the fort. He placed a finger on the map at the road to Saltillo. This was the main highway to the interior of Mexico. If reinforcements were on the way for Ampudia, they would come up the Saltillo road. "It ought to be blocked," Worth said.

"Yes," Taylor replied. "We don't have a battering train to hammer down their forts."

Down in Quitman's brigade there was so much enthusiasm over the coming fight that soldiers on sick report, who had been riding in the wagons, crawled out and reported for duty.

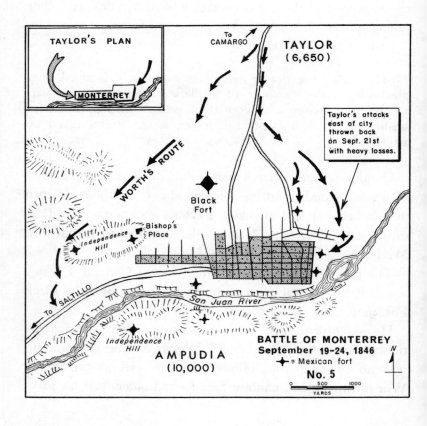

TAYLOR'S PLAN

MONTERREY

To CAMARGO

TAYLOR (6,650)

Taylor's attacks east of city thrown back on Sept. 21st with heavy losses.

WORTH'S ROUTE

Black Fort

Bishop's Place

Independence Hill

To SALTILLO

San Juan River

Independence Hill

AMPUDIA (10,000)

BATTLE OF MONTERREY
September 19-24, 1846
✦ = Mexican fort

No. 5

0   500   1000
YARDS

N

Hatless, General Quitman talked to his soldiers. His prominent forehead emphasized his earnestness:

Volunteers, we are now in the vicinity of the enemy. In an hour we may be called upon to face them in battle. Your spirit inspires me. I know your mettle, your impetuosity, and your recklessness of danger. There is no coward in my command. . . .

The volunteers screamed their reply. All they wanted was Quitman to lead the way.

Old Rough and Ready Taylor entrusted his main smash at the enemy to Haughty Bill Worth.* Worth was impetuous, a man capable of countermanding his orders in a twinkling. His leg wound from 1812 bothered him, but that was a brake he could overcome.

Taylor shook his hand and wished him Godspeed. That Sunday, at two o'clock in the afternoon, Worth and about two thousand soldiers cut around the Black Fort—well out of range.

The attack against the fortified city started. Taylor waited with Twiggs's and Butler's divisions back near the camp. Old Davy looked like anything but a Bengal Tiger; he felt ill.

Worth's soldiers worked their way through the dusty chaparral, through fields of sugarcane and grain. As an advance guard rode five hundred Texas Rangers under Col. Jack Hays. Behind the column rumbled three batteries of artillery and Captain Blanchard's Louisiana Volunteers—the rear guard.

In their haversacks the soldiers carried four days' cooked rations, but at the halts many filled themselves and tossed the haversacks, crowned with red blankets, aside. A haversack was

* The military historian, Col. John Elting, writes for this book: "Worth was a sort of cut-rate Winfield Scott. He was a fine fighter, tactician—when he stopped to think—and he made his soldiers behave. But he was twice as vain and touchy as Scott and about half as smart and as dedicated."

binding and uncomfortable under the arms and weighed you down in a fight.

It was seven miles the way Worth circled to the Saltillo Road. When his Rangers arrived, artillery on Independence Hill opened on them. Then night fell and rain came down in torrents. There was no place to take shelter from the storm, except some helped themselves by crowding into a group of *jacales*—crude huts belonging to peasants. Most of the soldiers spent the night in the drenching rain. They were miserable. Those who had food shared it, but by morning everyone felt hungry.

The day broke cold and overcast. The peaks of the mountains were lost in fog. Texas Rangers clattered out on the road again. Suddenly, out of the mist, a force of Mexican lancers charged them. For a moment the fight on horseback was anyone's battle. The Mexican leader was the brave Don Juan Najera. Edward Wallace wrote: "The Rangers were a bit impeded by carcasses of pigs and chickens they had requisitioned from the poor Mexicans."

Ben McCulloch and his Rangers reacted quickly, vaulting from their ponies. They took cover along a fence line and poured aimed fire into the lancers, who withdrew in disorder, leaving a hundred killed or wounded on the ground.

The noise of the cannonade from Independence Hill echoing in the mountains sounded like thunder. Quickly Worth sent soldiers clambering up the slope, and when they were halfway up a battery on Federation Hill across the river opened up. The attackers were caught in a cross fire. A cannon ball hit Captain McKavett, 8th Infantry, and cut him in two. In this crisis Worth ordered his main column out of range and told Capt. C. F. Smith to take two hundred Regulars and 140 dismounted Texas Rangers and ford the river to attack this new menace.

They waded the swift, cold stream under storms of grapeshot, holding muskets and rifles overhead. In some places the river was chin deep.

The situation looked desperate. General Taylor, seven miles away near the camp, was completely out of touch with the fighting. Worth saw the need for coordination. To get it, he sent a dragoon galloping to Taylor asking him to press the attack.

Shortly, Taylor and three regiments of infantry tried to fight their way into the east end of the town. They found the observations of the topographical engineers correct—every house seemed to be a fort. From behind sandbags on the flat rooftops and from behind the barricades in the streets, deadly fire decimated Taylor's men.

Back on the west side near the Saltillo road, Captain Smith's force struggled up the jagged rocks of Independence Hill under heavy fire from the top. Cannons at the summit could not be depressed enough to fire at the American attackers, but Mexican sharpshooters picked men off. It was hard for the soldiers climbing the slopes to hit targets at the top. Fighting uphill was slow, heartbreaking work.

To ensure the capture of Federation Hill, Worth sent the 5th Infantry Regiment and Blanchard's Louisianians across the river and up the cliffs as a second wave. Brigadier General Smith was the leader of this foray. The two Nicholls brothers, agile lieutenants from Louisiana, were scrambling ahead with the first wave.

The attackers overwhelmed the Mexicans on Federation Hill, who broke for the city. Not only did the Americans speed them on their way, but they seized two nine-pounders and turned them on Independence Hill. It was six hundred yards across the valley. Then the Americans raised their flag. Rain began to pour, but the flag flying from the redoubt on Federation encouraged the men fighting on Independence.

In the meantime, in Monterrey, Taylor's men were being mowed down. There were no decisive results. From every little orange grove, from every wall, from the rooftops, sharpshooters defended the town. Major Mansfield, out in front of the Texas Rangers, tried to find the best route, if any. Taylor sent into the city the 4th Infantry (six reduced companies) under Lt. Col. John Garland. Garland's sloppy instructions from Taylor were, "[Keep] . . . to the left. If you think you can take any of them little forts down there with the bayonet, you'd better do it. Consult with Major Mansfield. You'll find him down there."

Back near the camp close to town, with the mule train of the 4th Infantry, a small-sized lieutenant, regimental quartermaster, listened to the noise of the fight. This man, next to Abraham Lincoln, would do more than any other in saving the Union later in the Civil War.

2nd Lt. Ulysses S. Grant had had enough of the pesky mules and their problems. He had asked Colonel Garland for permission to fight and had been refused. Grant wrote in his *Personal Memoirs:*

At daylight the next morning fire was opened on both sides and continued, with what seemed to me . . . great fury. My curiosity got the better of my judgment, and I mounted a horse and rode to the front to see what was going on. I had been [in the city] but a short time when an order to charge was given, and lacking the moral courage to return to camp—where I had been ordered to stay—I charged with the regiment.

Grant also wrote that the charge was "ill conceived, or badly executed."

Captain Bragg ordered his cannoneers to follow the infantry into the streets. The battery galloped up, unlimbered, and began to fire into the houses at almost point-blank range. The noise was terrifying. Adobe dust from the buildings acted as a smoke screen covering men, horses, and guns. Musket fire wounded two of Bragg's horses. The battery had to withdraw; it was too close to the infantrymen. Lt. Sam French of New Jersey quickly unhitched the dying animals, and the guns were hauled to safety. The fight in the city grew hotter. The Mexicans on the roofs were slaughtering the American foot soldiers.

Bragg ordered young French back into the city. "Go save the harness off the dead horses," Bragg said.

French readied himself for this suicide mission. General Taylor rode up, saw French leaving, and halted him. "What's up?" Taylor asked.

French wrote afterward: "When the general found what I had to do he stopped me, saying, 'That's nonsense.'"

General Quitman led his brigade of Mississippians and Tennesseeans into the maelstrom in the eastern part of the town to help a regiment of Regulars. General Butler led the 1st Ohio Regiment in and fell wounded. Red-coated Mexican lancers charged in whirlwind style but were beaten back.

On Thursday morning Garland's regiment found itself out of ammunition. A message had to go at once to Taylor. It was too dangerous a mission, Garland said, to order anyone to perform. He asked for volunteers. Lt. "Sam" Grant volunteered. In his quiet style he wrote later: "My ride back was an exposed one."

Mounting a gray horse and fastening himself on the side of

the animal, crablike—Indian style—U. S. Grant started his horse at a run. Bullets cracked about him at the street corners. At the last intersection he braced himself without slowing the animal and cleared a four-foot wall.

In the meantime, to the west of the town, General Worth still had no orders from General Taylor. Messengers between the two had a six-mile ride, and when they arrived at the other end, they found themselves in unfamiliar terrain, with a battle raging. At night, the two American forces tried to communicate by firing rockets.

Later, in an official report that became a document of the Senate, Worth said, "Most of [my] troops were now 36 hours without food and were taxed to the utmost. They slept in the rain until 3 A.M. when they were aroused to go up *Independicia*."

Lt. George Meade and another topographical engineer led the way uphill through the cold drizzle, fog, and gloom. The rattle of the canteens of the Regulars alerted the Mexican sentinels, and a blaze of red flame greeted Worth's men. The combat became a stalemate. Lieutenant Roland, of Duncan's battery, and fifty infantrymen worked for two hours to muscle a howitzer and its ammunition up a hill about 750 feet high. They opened a plunging fire on the palace fort, and after a five-hour fight the Americans captured it.

When Worth's soldiers rushed into the palace redoubt, they gave an unearthly yell. Observers said later this was the first "rebel yell," which was to echo and reecho later on Civil War battlefields. Mexican bugles heralded a counterattack, but it was defeated. Haughty Bill Worth, a successful battlefield leader, could be stuffy when he took up a pen. He wrote: "In a few moments, the unpretending flag of the Union had replaced the gaudy standard of Mexico." Then, with more feeling: "We took care of our wounded and [gave] a decent interment to the dead, not omitting the enemy."

General Worth now was able to get hot food to his soldiers, their first in forty-nine hours.

Lieutenant Meade and Captain McCulloch scouted into the western half of the city and discovered that the Mexicans there had withdrawn to the main plaza. Battering rams, made from heavy timber, crowbars, and pickaxes helped Worth and two columns of men batter down doors and smash holes through the houses. His men were fighting like the Texans in 1836 at San Antonio—*through the walls of the homes.* Defending cannons blasted the attackers at across-the-street range. The noise, wreckage, and dust made this part of Monterrey a hell.

People of the town were pitiful and badly frightened. They had been told that the Americans would slay them in cold blood. They clustered about family altars. Captain Henry wrote: "They were on their knees, each with a crucifix." When he entered a house the cry was "Capitano! Capitano!" Women and children seemed delirious when they discovered they were not to be slain, and offered the Americans bread, oranges, figs, and other food.

Worth's two howitzers bombarded the cathedral and the plaza. The word was that the church held ammunition. Sharpshooters Worth sent to the roofs helped his soldiers fight to the center of the town.

When the Texans reached the roof of the post office, Mexican bugles blew and flags of truce came to the Americans. General Ampudia had had enough. The Americans felt thankful.

In the talks to agree upon an armistice, one of Taylor's representatives was Col. Jefferson Davis, leader of the Mississippi Rifles.

It was obvious that General Ampudia desired an interview with General Taylor. Taylor, fast becoming a hero in the United States, was painted in *Niles' National Register* of Baltimore as a picturesque warrior as fabulous as Andrew Jackson. The *Register* reported the interview:

Ampudia was all courtesy and fine words, big speeches, great volubility, with an abundance of gesticulations, shrugs, nods, alternate smiles and frowns, and that whole catalogue of silent language with which persons of French origin are wont to help the expressions of their ideas. General Ampudia is of a French family and was born in the West Indies.

Gen. Taylor, on the other hand, was as dry as a chip, as plain as a pipe-stem, and as short as pie crust. Dressed in his best coat, which by the looks had served some half a dozen campaigns, with his glazed oil cloth cap, strapless pants, and old fashioned white vest, looked more like an old farmer. . . .

Ampudia opened the interview by stating that his forces were too large to be conquered by General Taylor's army . . . that his loss was very small—but to spare the effusion of blood—to save the lives of helpless women and children—he was willing to compromise. . . .

Old Zack quietly stuck his hands deep in his breeches pockets, cocked his head a little on one side, and gently raised his grizly eyebrows . . . and replied, "Gen. Ampudia, we came here to take Monterrey, and we are going to do it on such terms as pleases us. I wish you good morning." And the old general hobbled off on his two short little legs, leaving the Mexican General and Staff in the profoundest bewilderment.

Although the conference between the two leaders accomplished nothing, other talks permitted Ampudia and his army to march away with most of their arms and equipment; there was to be no fighting for eight weeks.

When Ampudia marched his soldiers out of town with flags flying, drummers tapping out time, his soldiers looked amazingly clean in their gaudy uniforms and white crossbelts. Riding with a battery of field artillery, a green saddle-cloth on the back of his pony, came Ex-US Sgt. John Riley and other deserters. Riley sported a red coat with yellow epaulets. Grimy Americans lining the way screamed and hissed at the deserters, but Riley and his friends acted as if they did not hear. Next came a sad column of women and children, backwash of war.

While Ampudia's soldiers looked neat and soldierly, they felt angry at him and their other generals. They had lost confidence in their leaders and were worried over the future of their country.

Price of victory at Monterrey was 509 American casualties. Zachary Taylor, in his headlong smash into the eastern end of the city, was responsible for 84 percent of the killed and wounded. How many Ampudia lost is not certain. Probably he lost fewer men because he was on defense.

After this battle Taylor was not the hero to his men that he had been on the march along the Gulf. They recognized Worth as the better general. Lieutenant Meade wrote his wife: "General Worth will be the great hero." When Worth appeared on the streets, wild cheers went up, especially from the volunteers.

Finally the news reached the White House, and when the President heard that Taylor had allowed the Mexican soldiers to march away under protection of an eight-week armistice, President Polk became angry. He considered putting another general in Taylor's place, but lacked the courage because newspapers were writing Taylor up as *the* hero. The Whigs were talking, "Old Rough and Ready for President!" and Polk ever had an eye on voters.

It took seven weeks for the correspondence about the battle to travel from Taylor to Polk and back to Taylor, and when the general read the President's reply, it was his turn to become angry. The President wanted the armistice terminated at once. The Administration and others in Washington insisted on action.

But there was that word "logistics" again. An army needs smart, fearless battlefield leaders—poor ones can lose fights. However, you also must have ammunition, with more coming up, and other supplies such as food, shoes, medicines, uniforms, and trained reinforcements.

It is unglamorous to sit at a desk with pencil and paper and figure how many tons of ammunition are used in a day, how many tons must be on the road to resupply ammunition that is being expended—and like sums for every needed item. President Polk and many of his advisors lacked knowledge of logistics and of its significance. They just wanted Taylor to win the war.

10   BATTLE OF THE ARMISTICE

TAYLOR did not march south at once. He was having trouble, and not only with logistics.

Into his headquarters came a Mexican carrying his dying twelve-year-old son. Blood dripped to the floor. The father, in tears and almost struck dumb, offered his son as evidence of the conduct of the Americans. Taylor sent for the colonel whose men in the 1st Kentucky Volunteers had killed the boy, and told him angrily that his men had disgraced their state and the army. "Move out of the city and stay out," Taylor barked.

Holding the lid on the army, especially on the undisciplined volunteers, was hard for Taylor. A new arrival, one of the oddest officers in the army, Col. Ethan Allen Hitchcock—

The Pen of the Army, they called him, because of his high-flown writings on alchemy and philosophy—wrote in his diary:

Oct. 3, 1846—Since the arrival of the 2nd Dragoons there have been several disgraceful brawls and quarrels, to say nothing of drunken frolics.... One captain has resigned to avoid trial.... Two others are on trial for fighting over a low woman.

About the same time, Lieutenant Meade wrote his wife that the outrages of the volunteers were terrible. Capt. Benjamin S. Roberts made similar remarks in his diary.

The brawls of the Americans grew so bad that the governor of Monterrey sent a protest to Taylor. "No motive exists for the killings," the governor said. He noted, too, the difficulty in communicating with the American leader. The governor wanted to know if it would help if he used the French idiom.

Old Rough and Ready was in a quandary. He was not the best officer in the army at controlling soldiers—there had been disciplinary problems in the camps back along the Gulf at Corpus Christi. Taylor, with Perfect Bliss doing the phrasing, replied:

It is with sentiments of regret I learn your just cause of complaint. Your Excellency must be aware it is no easy task to keep such men in subjugation....

The volunteers will be removed in a few days. In the meantime Gen. Worth will use every measure to maintain order in the city.

I take the liberty to add that your Excellency has been misinformed in regard to my possessing knowledge of the French idiom.

Certainly Old Rough and Ready Taylor only specialized in the American idiom.

To occupy the volunteers, their officers drilled them long

hours with the Regulars, Capt. John Kenly writing: "The volunteers were pretty generally disgusted."

When reports of the atrocities first reached Washington, Gen. Winfield Scott drew up a paper, "Martial Law Order." It provided for trial and punishment for disgraceful acts committed abroad, but Secretary of War Marcy put it aside. "It's too explosive," he said.

To try to help Taylor, Scott sent a copy to him, but he tossed it aside, saying, "It's another of Scott's novels."

The really explosive issue in the United States was the unpopularity of the war. The word coming out of Mexico was that the Mexicans were far from beaten. To both sides defeat was unthinkable.

The President and his Cabinet talked of sending an expedition on the waters of the Gulf to attack the fortress at Vera Cruz.* General Scott ventured a gigantic idea: "Let's land there, attack the town, then march to Mexico City."

"How many soldiers would that take?" Polk asked.

"Between twenty-five and thirty thousand, sir."

Polk liked the idea but could not believe his ears. He felt Scott exaggerated. Nevertheless, he approved Scott's plan.

At this time, more infighting occurred. General Taylor wrote General Gaines, the Recruiting Genius, a private letter slurring the President and General Scott. The letter found its way to two New York newspapers. Polk was furious. Gaines eased the situation somewhat by saying it was a private letter addressed to him, but the President wrote in his diary: "The truth is Gen'l Taylor is in the hands of his political managers . . . he is unfit for command in Mexico. . . . I have no confidence in Scott, but I am compelled to send him."

* See Map No. 7, page 134.

The President did not realize that he was placing one of the most capable generals in our military history in overall command. The expert military historian, Col. John Elting, writes for this story:

As a military figure, I would rate Scott above both Lee and Grant, who fought later as generals. Scott was a professional soldier of the finest, most dedicated type. He trained himself to lead armies, and he trained armies that could be led to victory. No other American general spent the long, painstaking hours translating French manuals, learning how to feed men, how to care for their health, how to clothe and equip them. He could be brave in the old heroic style—up at the head of the attack, sword in hand. He could be quietly courageous, and he was always an effective soldier-statesman.

It was November 23, 1846, when Marcy gave Scott his written orders. The directive was amazingly broad. The strategy would be up to him; his operations would not be controlled, and he would be the judge of when to move. Polk showered him with attentions, and Scott felt happy and appreciative. The two conferred twice daily. Scott was assured that he would be backed with confidence.

The sixty-year-old general said to the President, "The best thing to do is to halt Taylor in northern Mexico. He can't possibly smash all the way to Mexico City. That's four hundred fifty miles. I'll go down there and see the general and explain I'm going to land an army at Vera Cruz and fight to Mexico City. I'll tell him to hold what he has, that I'll need some of his best units."

At this time and before it, Mr. Polk was talking secretly with his friend, Col. Thomas Hart Benton, able Senator from Missouri. Benton knew little about an army, but he was a Democrat from part of the Democratic party that was unruly. The charming and very ambitious Benton persuaded the President that *he* should command the landing against Vera Cruz and the expedition to Mexico City. Benton insisted that he be named a lieutenant general and promoted over Winfield Scott. It seemed to the President that this would unify his political party. In addition, the President had not forgiven Scott for a pithy letter he wrote: *"I do not desire to place myself in the most perilous of all positions: a fire upon my rear from Washington, and a fire in front from the Mexicans."* The President was double-crossing General Scott by his secret traffic with Thomas Hart Benton.

The next day the President and the general conferred again. Scott felt wonderful—he would have the President's backing. The general ordered his quartermaster to assemble supplies, munitions, and transports for his attack on Vera Cruz. Steam-propelled vessels had helped move soldiers in the Black Hawk and Seminole Wars. They would be used again but on a larger scale.

When Scott was leaving New Orleans on his way to see Taylor, he received upsetting news from a friend. The friend told him that the President had asked Congress to promote Benton so he could be given command of the venture. The news dumbfounded Winfield Scott. At first he refused to believe that the President could be so deceitful and shifty. Fortunately for the war effort and for the lives of the soldiers, congressmen thought the idea poor. Benton did not receive the job or the promotion.

Scott, although wounded temporarily in spirit, did not quit. He decided to push on to tell Taylor face to face—though he knew Taylor would erupt like a volcano when he heard that his part from now on would be minor and that his best regiments and some of his volunteers would be taken away for the landing at Vera Cruz.

In the meantime, Commodore David Conner, USN, and his Home Squadron in the Gulf were having adventures. This was the same seadog who refused to be stampeded at the Point Isabel base when young sailors, after hearing the noise of the battle at Palo Alto and after listening to a rumor of "Taylor's defeat," demanded to be allowed to go to the rescue.

It was hard work on blockade—weary hours on watch, the rough swell of the Gulf, and a long sail back to Pensacola for provisions and supplies. Conner had controlled his sailors at Point Isabel, but in August, 1846, young adventurers under Lt. James Parker of Ohio embarrassed him.

The trouble spot was on the coast not far from Vera Cruz— the old Spanish fortress of San Juan de Ulúa. Mr. Parker, USN, and a crew of midshipmen and sailors decided they could cut into the guarded waters after dark and seize the Mexican schooner *Creole*. At close range, the guns of the fortress frowned. It looked like suicide. The raiders' idea was to seize the ship and get away with it before the Mexican gunners knew what was up. The scheme collapsed, but in order to do some damage the raiders burned the *Creole*.

Commodore Conner felt like ripping up Parker but kept his temper. The raiders had no way of knowing that the schooner had served him as part of a secret scheme in communicating with US agents ashore.

In his headquarters at Monterrey, General Taylor felt angry when he received word from President Polk to break off the armistice with the Mexicans. It was ridiculous trying to run a war from Washington when that city and the battle front

were a half-a-world apart and communications slow. Taylor
thought he knew what was required, and most of his officers
agreed that an armistice was needed. Nevertheless, Taylor
carried out Polk's order. He sent dispatch riders to Santa Anna
telling him the armistice was over, that the Mexicans could
expect another fight. Then Taylor ordered Worth and his
division to Saltillo, seventy miles southwest of Monterrey.

At this time about a thousand Texas Rangers wanted to go
home. In his excellent book, *The Texas Rangers,* Walter Prescott Webb tells of their departure, with Taylor's permission.
Their enlistments were up, and word from Texas brought
news of fearful Indian raids. Taylor granted them leave with
mixed feelings; none surpassed the Rangers in courage, but in
the idle days of the armistice some of the Rangers had become
a problem, as they were lawless. "Fortunately Captain Ben
McCulloch promised Taylor, 'I will return.'"

Now, coming into Mexico with about two thousand soldiers
on a wide end run was a dependable soldier with unusual
characteristics.* This was Brig. Gen. John E. Wool of New
York, veteran of the War of 1812. He had been in the army
twenty-five years and had traveled in every state in the Union.
Some of his journeys in wild territory had been in the stern of
a birch-bark canoe, with an Indian swinging a paddle in the
bow.

Old Granny Wool, as his men called him, looked more like
a Harvard dean than a Regular Army general. The high blue
collar of his uniform gripped him about the throat as if it
were a rest for his chin. He was bald, and sensitive about it, so
he wore his hair on the side of his head brushed and plastered
in front of his ears. His nose was long enough to sniff out

* See Map No. 4, page 57.

trouble. He was clean and prim, and that was the way he wanted his soldiers. Prof. Justin Smith, who wrote one of the best histories of the Mexican War, said that Wool hated swearing, that if he himself slipped, "he would instantly raise his eyes to heaven and implore forgiveness."

Wool was not a glory chaser. Officers knew him as a quiet, competent professional. He had a reputation for bravery, for ability to organize, and as a fine administrator.

In late August, 1846, Wool had arrived at San Antonio just in time to fall heir to trouble involving Col. William Harney. Harney, noted both for bravery and for recklessness, had staged his own invasion of Mexico, without orders. He told his men after they crossed the border that he was going to ride all the way to Monterrey, but a number of the officers in his force of about five hundred men refused to follow him. Bill Harney had to be ordered back, but not before a fight in which his foolhardiness cost the lives of three men. The Mexicans gained prestige. Harney set his supplies on fire to prevent them from being captured and refused to turn his soldiers over to another officer, as ordered.

Wool, not the soldier to put up with such harum-scarum conduct, nailed Colonel Harney with court-martial charges.

Back in Washington, General Scott, who knew of Harney's reputation for bravery, straddled the situation by allowing Harney to pick the officers for the court that was to try him. As a result, the court only handed Harney a reprimand—then Scott forgave him. And before the court announced the sentence, Polk got into the act by praising Harney as "gallant . . . a Democrat in politics and one of General Jackson's personal friends."

Many in the city of Washington, particularly the army community, took a dim view of Scott's decisive but hard-to-under-

stand action. As for Polk, they understood him—he was first
and foremost a politician.

Sending Wool and his "army" of about two thousand to
make war in north-central Mexico was Polk's idea. Although
the army found no one to fight on its long march, eventually
the idea helped. Wool hiked to a place not far from Taylor;
in an emergency they could assist one another.

General Wool must have been glad to cross the Rio Grande.
With him rode the splendid Kentucky Mounted Volunteers,
spirited men. His 174-day march, much of it through rattle-
snake country dotted with cacti, covered over five hundred
miles. Maybe he marched as far as nine hundred. He was strict
and soldierly, and by the end of the march the green soldiers
with him knew how to take care of themselves.

Taylor said that Wool's march "accomplished nothing." At
that time Taylor did not know that Scott was coming to the
Rio Grande to take soldiers away from him for the vital
thrusts against Vera Cruz and Mexico City.

On the Gulf Coast, Commodore Conner now got a break.
A letter from Washington ordered him to capture the port
of Tampico, one of the best on the Gulf. The message fell
into Mexican hands, and when Santa Anna saw it he ordered
General Parrodi, commander of Tampico, to abandon the
place. This was in November, 1846. It seemed incredible to
Parrodi to surrender Tampico. In addition, it would take at
least eight hundred mules to carry away the most valuable
supplies so they would not fall into Conner's hands.

After Parrodi abandoned Tampico, Santa Anna ordered
him court-martialed for surrendering the area. The temperate
Mexican writer, Ramón Alcarez, wrote in 1850: "How could
Santa Anna expect Parrodi would be condemned when they

should have condemned the conduct of Santa Anna? . . . Parrodi was not the real culprit."Giving the American navy the port of Tampico proved to be a bad mistake.

It was Christmas week, 1846, when General Scott arrived at the river in order to tell Taylor he would have to weaken his army for the main push against Vera Cruz and Mexico City. Because Scott had sent a message ahead, he expected to meet Taylor. However, the dispatch rider, 2nd Lt. John Richie, one year out of West Point, met a foul end, and the message did not get through. When news of his death dragged back to the United States, *Niles' Register* reported:

FATE OF LIEUTENANT RICHEY [*sic*], USA—

Lt. R. belonging to the 5th Inf., was started with important despatches from Gen. Scott to Gen Taylor. For protection, the Lieut. had 10 Dragoons riding with him. They reached Monterrey safely. . . . Lt. R. whilst occupied in procuring something for the party and their horses to eat, crossing the plaza a Mexican on horseback whirled past, threw his *lasso* over Lieut. Richie and dashed off with his prize at full speed. A mile or two from the place, the lieutenant's body was afterwards found, stripped and dreadfully lacerated. His despatches fell into the hands of Mexicans. If we mistake not, Lieutenant Richie was of Ohio.

The papers in the dead lieutenant's leather dispatch case—a map and an outline of Scott's plans—were rushed to central Mexico to Santa Anna. This put the Mexican President-general in a position of knowing more about the war than General Taylor, and the Mexican leader quickly decided to take advantage of what he knew.

11   BATTLE AT BUENA VISTA

WHEN Santa Anna examined the papers and map captured from the unfortunate Lieutenant Richie and had satisfied himself they were genuine, he faced a decision. What was best? Should he march his army back to Vera Cruz to meet General Scott's invasion, or should he press north and attack Taylor, who would obviously become weaker with every man he sent to Scott?

The dictator made his decision and promised his soldiers victory. When he announced he would march north and beat Taylor, then return and defeat the *gringos* at Vera Cruz, his men reacted with enthusiasm. They followed him north, across a hump in the Sierra Madre Oriental and down its slopes to San Luis Potosí.* Here they found four thousand veterans of the battle of Monterrey. SA lost no time sending recruiters through the country with the word he needed thousands more to insure the defeat of the *gringos*.

In San Luis, at his order, up went shops, and work rushed ahead to equip his soldiers with swords, lances, muskets, ammunition, and uniforms. The people of the town labored to support his army. They, too, wanted to hurl the invaders back. In two months about 25,000 men camped in and about the town, awaiting SA's orders.

His enthusiastic men needed training in arms and field maneuvers, but he preferred parades and ceremonies. He and some of his top officers entertained beautiful women, and gossip drifted to the tents of the soldiers.

Now a newspaper from New York carried an article asking why President Polk allowed Santa Anna to return to Mexico. Could the wind be carrying a suggestion of treachery? Could Santa Anna be "President Polk's man"? His enemies spread the word that Santa Anna was interested in three things— money, money, money. Rumors circulated about Mexico that he was using government funds to gamble, that the money he was trying to raise would go for cards and cock fighting. There was a whisper in the camps at San Luis that in selecting officers he played favorites. This and the thought of the hard campaign ahead caused desertions.

Mexican newspapers placed pressure on Santa Anna. "Crush Taylor in northern Mexico," they demanded—and he agreed.

Three months was as long as he thought he could afford to stay at San Luis, although his army still needed food, clothing —and practice. He ordered his advance guard north. He had

* See Map No. 4, page 57.

about 24,500 men, and spies told him Taylor commanded only four thousand. It looked almost like a cinch. All he had to do was conquer geography and weather—march his army over the hard country to the north. The *gringos* would be outnumbered and overpowered. But conquering geography and weather can be most difficult.

The Mexican cavalry looked glorious as it swept out of San Luis. As General Miñón, leader of the two thousand horsemen in the advance guard, cantered by, he saluted SA with a flourish of his sword. Then followed the horse-drawn artillery, a company of engineers, and the San Patricio Battalion of American deserters. This was January 28, 1847.

It took three days for the army to move out. Santa Anna rode in the best place—the center, where he could communicate with his advance guard and with his supply train, such as it was. He relaxed grandly in his carriage drawn by eight white mules. Following close behind in carriages rode women, most of them of poor reputation. Then trotted five pack mules, crates of fighting cocks strapped to their backs.

Three hundred miles stretched ahead. Many writers have described the country the army marched through as desert. Actually it is semi-arid tableland, sliced with deep-cut ravines and rimmed with volcanic cones.

Wives of many of the soldiers were on the march; some even had their children along. Numbers of women burdened themselves with bundles of wood because they knew that soon wood for cooking would be hard to find.

On the twelfth day a norther enveloped Santa Anna's marchers. The temperature dropped to almost zero. Then it snowed. Men unused to such weather and to sleeping on the ground fell sick, unable to continue. The roadside became strewn with the sick, the dying, and the dead. Food supplies started to fail. Morale fell.

The snow changed to rain, and for two days the army marched in a drizzle. Gaps appeared in the columns as soldiers deserted. Santa Anna sent cavalry patrols after them. It meant a firing squad for men who were caught, but when food grew scarce and men became hungrier, every night more disappeared.

Now the sun came out and dried the earth and the puddles. Water became more precious than diamonds. At the water holes people struggled with each other to fill their gourds. The temperature shot up and dust storms half-blinded the marchers. SA rode up and down the long line, his magnetism and promise of victory keeping the march moving. When he appeared the soldiers shouted, "*Viva!*" and raised their weapons. To make food last longer, the general ordered the soldiers' wives back, but not all obeyed his orders.

A division marching in front stopped in a town for a rest, not notifying the division behind, and the road became jammed. When SA saw this he became furious and ordered the second division to countermarch fifteen miles. Morale fell, and men became worn out. By the time his army ended its fearful three-hundred-mile march, it had shrunk to fourteen thousand fearless, determined soldiers.

In the meantime, Scott was stripping Taylor of his best units as well as volunteers, for the thrust from Vera Cruz. Taylor felt discouraged. He wrote his son-in-law:

Things look gloomy. . . . We now begin to see the fruits [of an] intrigue by Marcy and Scott [against me]. . . . People expect me to leave the country in disgust & return to the U. States, but in this I shall disappoint them. . . . I will do my duty.

It was a bitter blow to have his best units and best fighter, General Worth, leave. About five thousand left Taylor on the 450 mile march to Tampico to join Scott.*

Winfield Scott had a special worry about the coming campaign to strike "the City," as Mexicans often called the capital. Articles appearing in the newspapers looked like ill omens. News of the planned landing was exciting copy. Nothing could be kept secret. *Niles' Register* even printed a description of the road from Vera Cruz to Mexico City and the towns along it, and discussed key terrain features. Back as far as October the New York *Herald* had talked of various schemes to win, and said, "The best passage to the Mexican capital lies through Vera Cruz."

The trek of some of the volunteer regiments from Taylor to the coast for the big push rambled almost like an election parade. Engineer 2nd Lt. George B. McClellan wrote of the "mustang cavalry" on its way to Tampico:

These volunteers rode long-eared jackasses, bought at a $3.00 to $5.00 rate. These men did not march with their companies. They procured Mexican saddles or rode bareback. Some of the donkeys were so small the riders had to lift their feet. The mustang cavalry straggled for miles—anything to avoid the discipline of the march.

McClellan detailed a conversation between two volunteers, one a lieutenant colonel, the other a private:

"Hello, there," said the colonel, who was disgusted with the angle at which the man kept his place in line, "you don't know how to file."

"The hell I don't," yells the man. "Damn you, I've been marching all day, and I guess I'm tired."

* See Map No. 4, page 57.

Back in the United States, Zachary Taylor was a hero. People were saying that he should be the next President. Small boys recited "poetry":

> "Old Zach's at Monterrey
> Bring on your Santa Anner,
> For every time we lift a gun
> Down goes a Mexicanner."

But in late February, 1847, Zach wasn't at Monterrey, and to neither President Polk nor General Scott was he a hero. Both had written him, "Hold what you have"; but he had no use for their advice and marched his men fifty miles deeper into Mexico to seize an important road junction.

When countrymen brought rumors that Santa Anna was marching north, Taylor pooh-poohed them. "Bosh!" he said. "How can an army get through that country, especially at this time of the year? How many horses, wagons, and pack mules would it take just to haul the food?"

The men liked Taylor; he was less jumpy than Worth. Once, back near Monterrey, Worth had believed a rumor that Santa Anna was coming and made his men make forced marches to get into a better position. The Grand Scare, they called it. Taylor, too, was more congenial. "I spent the evening with Genl. Taylor," Captain Roberts of the Mounted Rifles wrote in his diary, "and had a long and amusing talk upon the ups and downs of war & life in general—the more I see of Old Rough and Ready, the more I like the man."

But the general could be as stubborn as a mule. Twenty-two miles further south he marched his soldiers. He wrote later, "I marched deeper into Mexico this time to restore the confidence of my volunteers." It was an unusual way to restore confidence. Probably he was showing them that he believed in them.

Roberts noted: "The day has been hot and our marching fatiguing. We continued along the base of the mountains, through the loveliest part of Mexico—wild flowers & fruit in abundance . . . gardens of the *haciendas* filled with oranges, etc. We are camped tonight on a stream filled with trout. . . ."

He also wrote: "Santa Anna's 30,000 men cannot be kept long in idleness and in inaction. He is too shrewd for this."

Then the captain observed that no one in the United States Army knew what Taylor would do. His army was scattered. Suddenly, dragoons rode in with word, "Santa Anna's marching hard at us. His cavalry gobbled up some of our patrols." Now real worry set in.

North up the road thirteen miles, at a most unusual mountain pass, lay a ranch named Buena Vista. The country at the pass looked as if an angry god had rumpled it up. Not only did deep gulches, gullies, and a stream with steep banks carve up the land, but volcanic cones and a mountain range with many ravines frowned from the sides of the pass. When the earth was born, this place received special attention. Now the dirt road from San Luis Potosí wound through the center of the area as if it were trying to escape.

It was General 'Old Granny' Wool, who marched in with valuable reinforcements, who selected Buena Vista as a battle ground. Taylor said later the pass gave him gloomy thoughts of the ancient Greeks at Thermopylae.

Captain McCulloch and a handful of Texas Rangers galloped into camp and reported to General Taylor that they had scouted inside the Mexican lines. "Comin' straight at us," McCulloch drawled. "They have way over ten thousand.

Outnumber us three to one." After reporting, McCulloch and one of his Rangers rode fearlessly back to keep an eye on Santa Anna's men.

In the morning when the Mexicans broke their camp, smoke from their breakfast fires shrouded the country. Taylor, deeply concerned, decided to fight. He ordered his force to assemble near Buena Vista, and such stores as could not be hauled were to be put to the torch. Smoke from both fires screened his men.

When Santa Anna, who called himself the Napoleon of the West, learned the enemy was withdrawing, he leaped to the conclusion that Taylor was in full retreat to Monterrey, maybe to the Rio Grande.

The Mexican leader was delirious. His chief concern was that he might not catch the *gringos*. He led 2,500 horsemen and a handful of infantrymen in a dash up the road.

In spite of being hungry, his soldiers responded to his leadership. They were in high spirits. He promised them victory and loot—and that they would be the saviors of Mexico. He rode horseback gracefully although the saddle irritated his amputated leg. Smartly, he sent General Miñón and his horsemen on a wide sweep to the east to reach the American wagon train and to cut off the Americans' retreat. This could be the key to the battle. If General Miñón was successful, Taylor's 4,757 soldiers would be practically surrounded. "None must escape," Santa Anna shouted at Miñón.

When SA and his cavalrymen charged up the road, they stopped in front of the American position. Had they kept on they would have found the Americans unready.

There was some fighting on February 22, 1847. At dusk along the American outpost line, as a salute to the day, officers gave the password to the sentinels: "Memory of Washington."

Near the end of the day, out from the Mexican lines rode an officer and a sergeant, the latter bearing a white flag. The officer, a German named Van der Linden, surgeon general for Santa Anna's army, bore a note for General Taylor. While Taylor retired to his tent to read the letter by candlelight, Van der Linden, trying to impress the Americans, said several times that Santa Anna had *twenty-three generals* with him. This was hardly frightening news.

Santa Anna's note read:

You are surrounded by 20,000 men. [You will] be cut to pieces. But as you deserve from me consideration and particular esteem, I wish to save you from a catastrophe.... To this end you will be granted one hour's time to surrender....

SA closed with the phrase, "God and Liberty!"

With Perfect Bliss at the pen, Taylor declined and signed himself, "With high respect, I am, Sir, your obedient servant."

The breeze carried from the Mexican lines a chant: *"Viva Santana! Viva la Republica! Libertad o Muerte!"*

Bitter winds swept the pass that night. Men in both armies, sleeping on the ground with scanty cover, suffered, especially the Mexicans who were famished. The two forces were so close that when reveille drums at dawn beat the long roll summoning the Americans to ranks, they saw Mexican priests saying Mass.

Bands in each of Taylor's regiments struck up "Hail, Columbia"; then the musicians laid aside their musical instruments and picked up litters. During the battle they would carry wounded to temporary aid stations the doctors had set up. General Wool rode the lines, reminding his men of their long, weary marches. "Here at last," he said, "is the enemy you have been looking for." Every American regiment unfurled the American flag.

Capt. John Marshall Washington, field artilleryman, placed his battery in a vital position behind an embankment the Americans built to block the road. Nearby, Taylor sat carelessly on Old Whitey. Taylor trusted artillerymen now.

Down from the hills a scout galloped. He reported to General Taylor, "About a thousand Mexican cavalrymen up there in the hills—they got lances and machetes—are riding around us. They are getting in our rear to cut us off." At this bad news, Taylor turned the battlefield over to Wool and galloped to the rear with a squadron of dragoons, ordering Col. Jefferson Davis to bring his Mississippi Riflemen as fast as they could travel. Davis' men, wearing red shirts and white trousers, looked as if they were marching to a holiday parade.

Taylor thought he had Wool and his army in a strong position in the amazing mountain pass, but it was weak because it stretched but three thousand yards. It could be outflanked in the hills, and that was exactly what Santa Anna was doing.

The Mexican also ordered a division—General Blanco's—to smash straight ahead at Captain Washington's battery and against infantrymen close by. To stop the Mexican drive, Lt. John Paul Jones O'Brien dashed forward with his three horse-drawn cannons and went into action at close range. His horses and some of his gunners were shot down. O'Brien left his horse and served one of the pieces himself.

The brave Mexican division marched on and was slaughtered.

Santa Anna, excited, ordered in General Pacheco's division. His soldiers responded fearlessly, but they could not cross the gully and were routed. Santa Anna's piecemeal attack was helping the Americans.

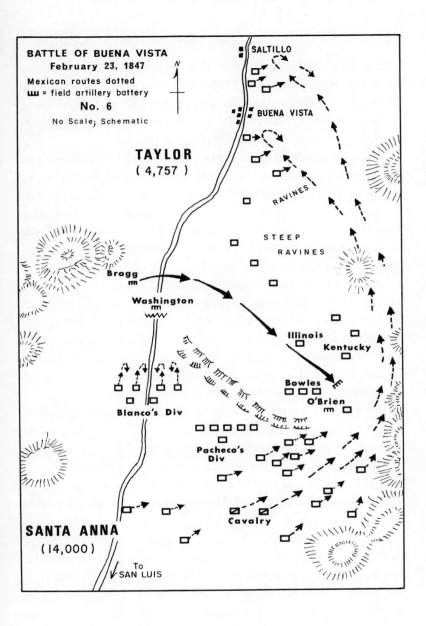

BATTLE OF BUENA VISTA
February 23, 1847

Mexican routes dotted
ɯɯ = field artillery battery

No. 6

No Scale; Schematic

N

SALTILLO

BUENA VISTA

TAYLOR
(4,757)

RAVINES

STEEP

RAVINES

Bragg
ɯ

Washington
ɯ

Illinois

Kentucky

Bowles

O'Brien
ɯ

Blanco's Div

Pacheco's
Div

Cavalry

SANTA ANNA
(14,000)

To
SAN LUIS

Scouts pointed out the American weakness: Not only was the enemy line short, but to the east near the mountains the ravines were not deep, and it was no trick to scramble down and out of them. Santa Anna led his foot soldiers in a concentration against the American left flank.

This movement to the eastern hills brought a crisis for the Americans. For some reason never made clear, Colonel Bowles of the 2nd Indiana ordered his soldiers to withdraw. In the Indiana ranks a panic developed. Arkansas and Kentucky mounted men thought all was lost, and fled with the Indiana men. Lieutenant O'Brien, all but overwhelmed, had to pull back, leaving a cannon for the Mexicans.

Fortunately, at this moment General Taylor returned from the rear. With him marched his dragoons and Col. Jefferson Davis' regiment of Mississippi Rifles. A panic on a battlefield is a hard thing to stop, but if anyone could end the stampede, it was Zachary Taylor. His dragoons, Davis and his Mississippians helped. The 2nd Indiana and the mounted men ended their flight, turned around, and resumed battle.

Illinois and Kentucky infantry, on the key flank, fought a vastly superior enemy force. Colonel Hardin of Illinois and Colonel McKee and Lieutenant Colonel Clay of Kentucky fell at the head of their regiments, mortally wounded.

In the whirlwind of the fight, the San Patricio Battalion, about 260 of them, manned Mexican field guns and pounded their former friends.

Just as SA ordered in his last division, a cannonball killed his horse. The fall hurt the Mexican's amputated leg, yet he quickly mounted an aide's pony. He straightened his uniform, and with a flourish of his sword pointed to the mountain range to the east. He was indicating, *There lies the path to victory.*

Now, when the Americans were almost exhausted, Captain Washington brought his guns to bear on Mexicans sneaking up a ravine. In a new charge, the Mexicans overpowered Lieutenant O'Brien's new position. He fired until the Mexicans were at the guns and until he had no gunners left. He managed to get back. Lt. George H. Thomas, an equally staunch fighter, was able to save the gun he commanded.

In this crisis, Capt. Braxton Bragg ordered his battery to leave its position on the west side of the road. Bragg galloped with his guns across the road straight at the Mexicans. It looked as if Bragg and his cannons were charging for a hand-to-hand battle. Suddenly the battery wheeled. In a twinkling the tired cannoneers unlimbered their guns and poured canister into the Mexicans. A survivor of Bragg's outfit wrote: "They were just a few yards from the muzzles." The story arose that at this moment General Taylor said, "A little more grape, Captain Bragg." Actually Taylor shouted, "Double-shot your guns and give 'em hell!"

The key action of the field artillery in the crisis proved too much, and SA's disappointed soldiers left the field.

General Miñón's cavalry—what was left of it—now rode back from its attack on the American rear, a failure to report. Miñón's horsemen arrived just in time to join Santa Anna's retreat.

Taylor's army felt thankful that it had not been crushed, that it could remain on the battlefield. Colonel Bowles' order which caused the panic was not the result of cowardice. His men knew him to be brave, but he was green and confused. The Americans lost 740 in killed, wounded, and missing.

Santa Anna's piecemeal attacks led to his defeat. They let Taylor shift batteries and regiments. SA's faulty generalship cost his country between fifteen hundred and two thousand soldiers in killed and wounded, as well as its high hopes of victory. Most of his beaten men now saw him in his true light —an inspirational adventurer who lacked character and professional knowledge. Following him proved worse than chasing an evil will-o'-the-wisp.

12   THE ROAD BACK

AFTER the desperate fight, the irony of war was demon-
strated on the battlefield: Americans shared their hard-
tack and water with wounded Mexicans and gave them first
aid.

It was horrible for the Mexicans on the road back to San
Luis Potosí. There was no transportation for Santa Anna's
wounded. The Mexicans started carrying them, four men to
a hastily made litter, but you can't carry wounded men three
hundred miles on stretchers when food supplies are low. Dear
friends had to be abandoned to the wolves and wild dogs who
prowled just out of rifle shot. Some women refused to leave
wounded husbands, and starved. At the first water hole, a
slimy pond covered with green scum, children were thrust

aside as thirst-crazed men rushed into the water. Some died from drinking too much of the foul liquid.

Santa Anna decided that he would leave his army to struggle back under Ampudia, while he rushed to San Luis with his staff to see about supplies, to check on political affairs, and to spread the news of "victory." He did not possess the character to stay with his suffering men. Staff officers could have ridden back to gather food and to make arrangements for the wounded, but the general said this was *his* mission.

No sooner had he departed than discontent spread among the men. Few believed Ampudia competent, and the army started falling apart.

At each town on his long ride to the rear, SA displayed two captured American flags and three small American cannons. Boastfully, he crowed, "These flags and guns are proof of our great victory." He explained he was rushing back to get needed supplies and to provide for the wounded, that he had cavalry watching General Taylor. The truth and Santa Anna were complete strangers.

Later, he hedged some, writing his friend General Vasquez:

Blood ran in torrents, both armies lost 3,000 or 4,000 men in killed and wounded. Our bayonet charges resulted in the death of hundreds. . . . Treason prevented me from gaining a complete victory. A native Mexican soldier deserted . . . and informed General Wool of my approach. General Wool quickly struck his camp . . . and occupied the impregnable position which it was impossible to reduce.

General Miñón, the cavalry leader, wrote the newspaper *Independiente* two months later, extolling the bravery of the Mexican soldiers and describing the piecemeal attacks:

The battle was nothing but an unconnected succession of sublime individual deeds—partial attacks of several corps. . . . There was no methodical direction, no general regulated attack ... no plan in which the efforts of the troops could produce a victory....

⟨ Not long after the battle, General Taylor withdrew to Monterrey, where he stayed for months, functioning as a military governor. ⟩

In the story of the United States Army up to this time, no such victory can be pointed out. At Buena Vista, Taylor and his men successfully resisted an enemy three times as large. They had been helped by Santa Anna's poor generalship, but in the teeth of huge odds they refused to be pushed from the battlefield. However, in fighting instead of withdrawing, Taylor had gambled the American war effort, for if he had been defeated General Scott would have been recalled from the Gulf to save Texas.

Although the President thought the battle unnecessary, he sent Taylor his congratulations. When news of Buena Vista reached the citizens of the United States, excitement spread. This victory eventually swept Old Rough and Ready Taylor into the Presidency. When he arrived in the States in late 1847, relieved at his own request, he received a hero's welcome.

The American people relished stories of the battle. Newspapers praised the coolness and the bravery of the Mississippi, Illinois, and Kentucky soldiers. The story was told of how, in the panic, Colonel Bowles, instead of running, seized a rifle and joined the Mississippians. The heroism of Braxton Bragg and Jefferson Davis was told and retold. Just before the crisis of the fight a bullet struck Davis in the foot and, being unable to walk, he ordered that he be carried to the front in a wagon.

Two of the hated San Patricio Battalion were captured.

"What shall we do with them?" officers asked General Taylor. "Let's hang 'em!"

Americans who had suffered from the deadly fire of the San Pat deserters felt Taylor was too kind, because he ordered them released and drummed beyond the lines to the tune of the "Rogue's March." Many felt that before the war ended severe punishment should be dealt to the entire battalion of traitors.

When Col. John Hardin's body was buried at Jacksonville, Illinois, five months after the battle, fifteen thousand people honored his memory by attending.

An equally heartrending funeral was given Capt. George Lincoln of Worcester, Massachusetts. Lincoln, son of a governor of Massachusetts, was known throughout the state as "the Bayard of the American Army" because of his knightlike fearlessness. He had fought as a member of the Kentucky Volunteers. When the special train bearing his body chugged into Worcester, all work stopped. The stores closed. The entire population of the town mourned and joined the funeral cortege.

Crossed on his coffin lay two swords belonging to the young captain. Behind the caisson bearing the flag-draped coffin, a dragoon led the horse which Captain Lincoln had ridden at Buena Vista. The saddle was empty. Two black boots, facing to the rear, rode the stirrups. Two bands, spaced in the procession, played music that reminded the townspeople of Captain Lincoln's devotion to his religion and to the country. It often appears in combat that the men who turn the battle are the ones who are lost.

13 NEW MEXICO AND CALIFORNIA— KEARNY AND DONIPHAN

In the meantime one of the best officers on the western frontier received strange orders at Fort Leavenworth, Kansas. This was Col. Stephen Watts Kearny (who pronounced his name "Carney").

In mid-1846, Mr. Marcy sent this expert on Indians and the country between the Missouri and Mississippi Rivers critical instructions: *"Seize and hold New Mexico.... Press forward to California.... If you conquer and take possession of New Mexico and California you will establish temporary civil governments...."*

No other colonel in the story of the US Army has received such weighty orders.

Kearny, vigorous and intelligent, had the background and character to carry out such an extraordinary mission. Born in Newark, New Jersey, he was a veteran of the War of 1812 and noted for his force. Later, when trouble developed, particularly in California, Kearny must have read and reread his unusual orders.

He knew the situation in New Mexico. Governor Armijo, an adventurer, ruled with a clutch of steel in untrustworthy fashion, and others in power in New Mexico reflected his corruption. It would be an error to call Armijo's administration a government.

President Polk and thousands of Americans hungered to enlarge the United States. Politicians and newspaper editors gave this desire to expand a high-sounding but meaningful phrase: They called it *Our Manifest Destiny*. The marvelous San Francisco Bay and the country around Los Angeles glittered like prize jewels. Polk once hoped to buy California, and he was determined that no European power would take it.

The man he selected to lead dragoons to California could be intense. When Stephen Watts Kearny gave an order, he wanted it carried out. But he understood people and enjoyed humor. Once on a horseback trip into wild territory in 1820 he described an Indian guide and his wife, who carried a four-month-old papoose on her back. Kearny wrote:

The dull monotony of traveling over the Prairies is occasionally interrupted by the feats of *Horsemanship* shown by our squaw, & the affection & gallantry shewn toward her Papoose by the Indian Guide.

Four of our party went in pursuit of a *gang of elk*. . . .

[Later when the guide lost his way] the squaw has been weeping piteously [afraid that] we should *play Indian* with her husband, sacrificing him on the altar of his ignorance. A plate of soup and some kind words [quieted both of them].

When word went out that Colonel Kearny would lead into New Mexico and California, hundreds of young men eager for adventure flocked to Fort Leavenworth from Missouri, Ohio, Illinois, Kentucky, Tennessee, and Mississippi. When he started in June, 1846, his "Army of the West" stretched for miles along the Santa Fe Trail, although it numbered only 1,658 soldiers.*

Adding to the length of his column of horsemen and a few infantrymen, rolled his covered wagons. Then behind a mule-pack train toiled the wagons of frontiersmen, settlers, and hunters. The total number of animals reached almost fifteen thousand.

Up in front rode the colonel, with about 150 Shawnee and Delaware Indian scouts. Jogging a day behind the "army" rode a natural leader, Alexander Doniphan, tall, red-headed frontier lawyer elected as a colonel by his Missouri Volunteers. They loved him—all they desired was for Colonel Doniphan to tell them what to do.

Hiking twenty-four to thirty-two miles a day, day after day, in any kind of country is hard. Your feet become sore and your bones weary. Your pack feels almost like a cross. The trail to the four hundred-year-old capital of New Mexico, Santa Fe, wound over bad lands where water was scarce and where sometimes dust storms tortured the marchers. Far to the front, as an advanced point, with twelve horsemen and a flag of truce, rode a West Point captain from Leesburg, Virginia, Philip St. George Cooke. Indians hit Kearny's trains and drove away cattle; still he marched on.

* See Map No. 4, page 57.

Kearny, now a brigadier general, hoped to treat with Governor Armijo, but word came from friendly Indians that the people of New Mexico were rising at Armijo's call. This did not ring true, because Armijo had fleeced them. But American residents and officer scouts rode in with the alarming word for Kearny of a "Mexican army about twelve thousand strong, two thousand well-armed. The other ten thousand carry bows, arrows, slings, and clubs." Rumors said this citizen army waited to pounce on his column from a fine defensive position at Apache Canyon, near Taos.

This force could not be disregarded. But before Kearny made up his mind as to what to do about Apache Canyon, scouts trotted in with a Mexican soldier from a Santa Fe outpost. The soldier told Kearny, "Señor general, there is no danger. Armijo's army has gone home. Maybe to hell. The canyon is clear."

Kearny's hard side boiled to the top. "If you are lying," he said, "I will hang you." Fortunately the soldier was telling the truth. Armijo and his army had disappeared.

On the fiftieth day of the hike, August 18, 1846, Kearny's Army of the West with nine hundred miles behind them, walked in the rain into Santa Fe. Its officers and men felt thankful there was no opposition. Immediately Kearny claimed the country for the people of the United States. He assured the citizens of the city, "The United States will protect your persons, property, and religion. We will not take an onion or a pepper without paying the full equivalent in cash." No one could back up his word more firmly than Stephen Watts Kearny.

In Santa Fe, he pressed the work so his soldiers could ready themselves for the march to California. He asked Colonel

Doniphan and another lawyer in the Missouri Volunteers, Pvt. Willard P. Hall, to draw up a constitution for the government of New Mexico. Doniphan and Hall teamed well; they drew heavily from the Declaration of Independence and the American Bill of Rights.

"We will protect your persons, property. . . ." Kearny had promised the people of New Mexico. To them this meant protection against Indians. When Doniphan finished his writing, Kearny sent him against the Navajos and Apache raiders, and Doniphan signed a treaty of peace with Navajo chiefs.

Then, before Kearny started his hike for California, he sent Doniphan into north-central Mexico to team with Old Granny Wool. This caused the big redhead to lead his Missouri Volunteers on one of the most extraordinary marches in the story of the American people.

The astonishing march started in December, 1846. The first problem Alexander Doniphan met was waterless country, ninety miles of it.* To cross the desert, everything that would hold water was filled—even the scabbards of the officers' sabers—so his soldiers could survive the three-day hike over arid land.

Doniphan's 856 Volunteers believed that as long as he was with them they could do anything. Their first brush with the enemy came at El Paso, and it proved a mere skirmish. So with little trouble they occupied the town nestling beneath the Franklin Mountains.

After marching south across more desert wastes, they won the next battle against great odds. Over four thousand Mexicans waited for them at the Sacramento River on high ground, behind twenty-eight redoubts (small forts) and a line of

* See Map No. 4, page 57.

trenches. Before the fight, about thirteen antelopes bounded across the front of Doniphan's marching men. The Americans needed food, and their rifles brought the antelopes down. It was an astonishing display of markmanship, at the right time.

In the hard fighting, everything seemed confused. This was a "first fight" for both sides, but the Mexican soldiers had received little training. The result was about three hundred Mexicans killed and one American. The capital of the Mexican state of Chihuahua fell to Doniphan the next day.

This march—to join Old Granny Wool's army—was hard. Doniphan's soldiers overcame heat, dust, thirst, distance, and fatigue. Part of the time they hiked on half rations through country where "ears of corn grew thickly and invitingly around them." The redhead told his men not to take corn that did not belong to them, and they carried out his orders.

Since General Wool was not where they expected, they marched on to Zachary Taylor at Monterrey; then, after a stay with him, north to the Rio Grande, down that river to the Gulf of Mexico where they sailed to New Orleans and to St. Louis. At St. Louis each Volunteer was welcomed "by hand." Senator Benton made a speech praising "Missouri enterprise, courage, and skill." In a year, Colonel Doniphan's men had marched an unbelievable 3,600 miles—three thousand of them over mountains and desert country.

Kearny and his men faced an adventure of their own. In late September, 1846, they started for California. *California!* The historian Samuel E. Morison wrote: "The very name meant mystery and romance." At this time only about fifty thousand people lived in California, about six thousand of them white. Even so, *"Press forward to California. . . . If you conquer . . . you will establish temporary civil government.*

. . ." was an extraordinary order for a general backed by only three hundred dragoons.

But before Kearny left New Mexico for California, he had a problem to solve that did not involve people. On the hike from Fort Leavenworth many of his horses had given out. His infantrymen had laughed at the dragoons and their horses as they marched by them. Obviously, horses were not rugged enough for the eight hundred hard miles stretching to California, so Kearny placed his men on mules. Everyone knew mules were smarter than horses and that they could keep going where horses tired. Kearny himself rode a saddle mule.

Behind Kearny and his tiny force traveled a Mormon battalion under Cooke, now a lieutenant colonel. Cooke described his Mormons in the wilderness:

Some [men and women] were too old—some feeble and some too young. The battalion was . . . worn out by traveling on foot from Illinois, its clothing scant. . . . Several oxen hauling the wagons fell and had to be rolled out of the road, the feet of others bleeding.

Seventeen days out of Santa Fe, on October 6, 1846, the two dragoons riding in front of General Kearny's party raised their rifles and signaled, *Enemy in sight!* The general quickly deployed his men, ready to fight, but the dust cloud in the distance turned out to be Kit Carson and a tiny group, including six Delaware Indians. Kit Carson—scout, trapper, and explorer—known throughout the West, had once been engaged as a hunter to supply Bent's Fort on the Santa Fe Trail with buffalo meat. He was illiterate but of undoubted integrity. His fabulous endurance enabled him to stand the severe tests of trips across the country in quick succession.

"I'm on my way to Washington with dispatches," Carson

said. "Come eight hundred miles and darned near starved, all of us."

The frontiersman let Kearny read the dispatches. The general was astounded. California, the messages said, was under the control of Commodore Stockton, USN, who was helping Lieutenant Colonel Frémont of the US Army Topographical Engineers set up a government. "We have the flag flying in every port," Kit Carson said. "California has surrendered."

Some men might have turned around, but not Stephen Watts Kearny.

Although the scout wanted to continue to Washington on his mission, the general persuaded him to send the dispatches to Washington by others and to lead the way back over the wastelands to San Diego, California. Carson agreed, although he was disappointed; he yearned to see his wife and family in New Mexico.

With a reduced "army," because of the scarcity of food, General Kearny pushed on—to trouble.

At this time the Mexican grip on California was weak, not only because of the distance and poor communication, but because of revolutions and turmoil in Mexico. Nevertheless, Mexican forces fought Kearny at San Pascual, not far from the Pacific Ocean at San Diego.

Colonel Kearny's scouts, working in the night, unintentionally alerted Mexicans and Indians in the village of San Pascual, and in their haste to get away the scouts dropped a blanket marked US. The enemy under Andrés Pico knew something was up.

This was a crisis. Kearny, within forty miles of San Diego, was blocked. It was all or nothing. To solve the dilemma, he ordered a before-dawn attack. Several historians have criticized his attack as rash, because Kearny was not sure of the size of the enemy force in San Pascual. In war you are seldom certain of the strength of the enemy against you, and in the cavalry tactics of the day, a charge was considered the best way to clear up a vague situation and to gain victory. It required quickness and courage.

In this dashing, close-quarters' fight, Kearny and twelve others were wounded, and after the fight his "army" buried eighteen of its soldiers. Had it not been for Kit Carson, Lt. Edward F. Beal, USN, and a third person—who might have been Alex Godey, noted scout, or a Delaware Indian— Kearny's men would probably have been overpowered in the next few days. The three men saved the day by crawling long miles in the sand through cacti to bring help from San Diego.

Now trouble began on the American team. A strange tug-of-war started: Kearny against Stockton and the impetuous explorer, Frémont. The characteristics of the three and Kearny's determination to carry out orders caused trouble.

Commodore Stockton, politically minded, overly ambitious, and not the brightest officer ever in command of an independent naval mission, was as impulsive as John Frémont.

They called Frémont the Pathfinder because of his explorations. His reports of these travels, written with the help of his wife Jessie (daughter of powerful Senator Thomas Hart Benton of St. Louis) who was exceedingly ambitious for her husband, did a great deal to interest people in the West. Frémont was an odd person, far more of an adventurer than a soldier. To this unique individual the conquest of California meant little more than an opportunity to gain personal fame and fortune.

No one was happier than he when the commodore appointed him governor of California, but he soon ran into difficulty: The civil government Stockton organized could barely function.

General Kearny's arrival in California brought on a serious Army-Navy clash. When he presented his orders from President Polk, Commodore Stockton acted haughty; he refused to recognize Kearny's authority. The mix-up was spiced by Frémont's personal hatred of Kearny. The Pathfinder looked upon him as a block on his trail to fame. To worsen matters, Frémont created friction among the various American soldiers in California and also between Americans and native Californians.

The confused state of things would have tried the patience of a saint. Kearny held onto himself and awaited the arrival of reinforcements from the East.

In February, 1847, Stockton was replaced by Commodore Shubrick, who sided with Kearny. Late that month, the experienced Col. Richard Mason arrived from Washington with orders saying that Kearny had the backing of the President, so Kearny went to work and set up an efficient civil government. There was trouble over land titles and over pay for Frémont's men.

An ordinary mortal would have given in, but not Frémont. He flew into a rage and challenged Colonel Mason to a duel. Mason accepted and named the weapons: double-barreled shotguns at close range, loaded with buckshot. Kearny saved at least one life by forbidding the fight.

Once, at drill back in Kansas, Kearny's horse had fallen with him. Although tangled with the reins, stirrups, and the horse, Kearny shouted at his soldiers, "Forward!" It was part of his nature to see that affairs always proceeded.

When he had done all he felt he could do in California, at the end of May, 1847, he left Mason as governor and started the long overland march to Kansas. With him, feeling like a prisoner, rode Lieutenant Colonel Frémont.

At Fort Leavenworth, Kearny placed the Pathfinder before a court-martial, charging him with mutiny and other crimes. The court pronounced Frémont "guilty of all three charges" and sentenced him to be dismissed from the service.

But his powerful father-in-law, Senator Benton, arranged for publicity that made the Pathfinder a martyred hero. President Polk, under unusual political pressure, declared John Frémont not guilty of mutiny but guilty of lesser charges, and "saved his face" by restoring him to duty. Soon Frémont resigned from the Army.

Senator Benton, who carried a grudge like an elephant, remained hostile to Polk and Kearny.

Because of Benton's animosity, Stephen Watts Kearny, superb and unusual leader, occupies an obscure place in history.

14   VERA CRUZ

O^N the Gulf a crisis was developing.

Scott, after having his repeated suggestion to the President approved—to land at Vera Cruz and fight inland to "the City"—saw himself as the best qualified general to command the expedition. This suited Mr. Marcy. The Secretary of War saw the burden of war direction lifted from his shoulders. He felt happy over the President's decision.

Tears filled Scott's eyes when President Polk informed him that he had been chosen as the invasion leader.

Now the war took on a broader scope, and at the same time Winfield Scott faced the critical stage in his career. If he failed, great numbers of his soldiers would die, he would be disgraced, and his country's efforts would be set back.

Scott calculated he needed 25,000 soldiers, but by no stretch of the imagination could the President envision 25,000 soldiers in Mexico. Mr. Polk allowed him only 13,000.

To succeed, Scott would first have to conduct successfully the hardest of military operations—landing on a hostile shore. Then he would have to cut through mountainous country that favored the defenders and supply his army over a long line that could easily be cut in pieces. If the landing succeeded, it could be Scott and thirteen thousand against a nation of seven million—maybe his invading army would unify the Mexicans, no one knew.

In the War of 1812, when a bullet thudded into his side at Lundy's Lane, his future lay in the balance, but he had recovered in a Philadelphia hospital. Now in March, 1847, his career again hung in the scales.

It was impossible to determine the odds against him and his tiny army. The answer to the question, "Where is Santa Anna's army?" might determine his chances.

Scott got under way.* One hundred and twenty miles north of Vera Cruz, on Lobos Island, he crowded his soldiers into sixty ships, most of them schooners built to carry freight. Fortunately for Scott (and for Taylor in his campaigns) Mexico had no navy.

Steam vessels puffed about the American fleet. Leaning over the rail of a schooner stood 2nd Lt. U. S. Grant. He wrote later in his *Personal Memoirs:*

These little steam propeller despatch boats—the first of their kind ever seen by anyone then in the army . . . little [side-wheelers] going through the fleet so fast, so noiselessly . . . propellers under water out of view, attracted a great deal of atten-

* See Map No. 7, pages 134–135.

tion. [When one thrashed by] Lieutenant Sidney Smith...
exclaimed, "Why, the thing looks as if it was propelled by force
of circumstances."

Down the coast sailed the fleet, the steam vessels with Scott's
headquarters ship, *Massachusetts*, in the lead. Aboard the
transports life was rough because soldiers and equipment were
jammed into the holds.

Off Vera Cruz lay part of the Navy's blockading fleet.
Living on the transports was simple compared to hazardous
work in the blockade. Boredom, long hours on watch with
little excitement were the enemies. Then when excitement
occurred the action was often unpredictable.

Back in December, Midshipman Rogers of the US Brig
Somers had gone ashore on a scout. Suddenly a squall cap-
sized the brig while she cut through the water in pursuit of a
strange sail out of Vera Cruz. Of the seventy-six on board the
Somers, thirty-nine lives were lost. To complete the unfortunate picture, Mexicans captured Midshipman Rogers.

Now the seadog Commodore Conner gave the American
general his ideas on where to land, and to look over the problem Scott and his principal officers boarded a tiny steamer
which American sailors had captured. Guns barked at the ship
from the huge fortress of San Juan de Ulúa, standing guard on
a reef at the entrance to the harbor. On the little vessel as
staff officers for Scott were Robert E. Lee, George Gordon
Meade, P. G. T. Beauregard, and Joseph E. Johnston; each
would become famous in the American Civil War.

After the reconnaissance, General Scott felt he could make
it. Infantry patrols he sent ashore at a beach three miles south
of Vera Cruz found no enemy. However, if Mexicans were
hidden, and if they charged out of the jungle to meet the in-

vaders at the water's edge, there would be chaos for the Americans and probably failure.

Before the landing Scott cruised through the fleet, a magnificent figure in full-dress blues, a gaudy yellow sash hugging his waist, his huge sword hanging from his belt. He towered above his staff officers. Excited soldiers on the transports, anxious to see action, cheered. Scott touched his hand to his fore-and-aft hat. He was really the captain of the team.

Down into the sixty-five surf boats clambered the soldiers, seventy men to a boat. From the stern of each little vessel flew the Stars and Stripes. The sea was as smooth as glass, with breakers pounding lazily on the beach. A light-blue sky seemed to stretch forever. The city and its fortress on a reef glistened beautifully in the sun, but there was danger there, and to avoid it Scott ordered his soldiers landed out of range of the Mexican guns. This was March 9, 1847.

Four or five schooner-rigged gunboats escorted the surf boats as close as possible to the shore. Bands played "The Star-Spangled Banner." A cannon from the steamer *Massachusetts* roared as a signal. The surf boats started toward the shore in a long line, sailors rowing some, steamboats towing others. Cannons from the gunboats thundered at the jungle, firing over the boats. The navy and the army were working together like a well-drilled team.

When the first surf boat grated on the sand, General Worth stepped out into the waist-high breakers, his sword drawn, and led the dash to the top of the beach. Hundreds of soldiers, bayonets fixed, followed him. Mexicans failed to meet them; not an American was lost. There were two other landings, and by ten at night Scott had ten thousand men ashore.

Serious problems still had to be solved.

To strike for Mexico City, leaving an enemy fortress and

four thousand soldiers in his rear, would not be smart. Now as his soldiers surrounded Vera Cruz, a norther howled, and cold rain drenched the Americans. In three months, maybe less, there would be no northers, but with heavier rains and hot weather the terrible *vomito* would increase. In 1847, no one realized that cool winds kept the yellow-fever rate low by blowing mosquitoes out to sea.

Obviously the army had to move inland before the yellow-fever season. Haughty Bill Worth favored rushing Vera Cruz in a bayonet attack, and several officers agreed with him. But Scott disapproved. He knew this was the sensational thing to do, but he was anxious to take the city and at the same time conserve the lives of his men. He considered besieging the town—starving it into surrender—but that would take time, so he decided on bombardment.

Commodore Conner and his sailors labored to bring the monstrous naval guns over the beach, difficult to do because the clumsy wheels were designed for short movement aboard ship. While the gunners were readying themselves, Scott considered other questions. Scouts brought word about bandits lying in ambush. But there were far more vital problems. Some of the animals belonging to the dragoons had been lost in the landing. Where could he buy more? Also he needed pack mules and animals to pull wagons.

Scott and the army suddenly felt better—wonderful news arrived of General Taylor's victory at Buena Vista. However, this brought on a new worry: What would Santa Anna do now?

Immediately after the landing General Scott, taking no chances, sent some of his soldiers inland to block the road to Mexico City so Santa Anna could not surprise him.

Many US soldiers had not been paid regularly, and when

money arrived from the States, Scott sent it up the road. He did not want to pay his men in Vera Cruz. Captain Roberts wrote his wife of his unusual job:

Jalapa, March 15, 1847

I am fatigued to death by the toil and the care of bringing up an immense train from Vera Cruz. . . . I brought up half a million for the Pay Master, and having been paid for April, I send you $100. . . .

In the meanwhile, the attack on the city of Vera Cruz began when General Pillow's brigade of Tennesseans, Pennsylvanians, and Regulars captured a powder magazine in the rear of the city. Robert Patterson, a veteran of the War of 1812, now a major general of volunteers, and Generals Quitman, Twiggs, and Worth placed their soldiers in a ring about the walls of the city. Ships of the navy eased into position where they could fire at the fortress.

Scott was ready to demand *Surrender!* when Padre Jarauta led fighting Mexican irregulars out of the jungles. Scott swept them aside. Now he sent into Vera Cruz a flag of truce with a message to General Morales. "Surrender!" it said, "and save blood and the beautiful city."

The answer from Morales was in keeping with his reputation for bravery and determination: "General Scott, let the operation of war commence in the manner you consider most advantageous."

The American bombardment started. Shells howled into Vera Cruz and exploded in its streets. A surgical hospital caught fire. Doctors and nurses carried patients to the Hospital of San Francisco. Soon it also went up in flames. A Mexican flag, its halyards cut by gunfire, fluttered down on one of the ramparts guarding the city. Through a shower of American fire and grenades ran 1st Lt. Don Sebastian Holzinger. He risked his life to rig his flag back up.

Commodore Matthew C. Perry,* gunnery expert—Old Bruin, his sailors called him—now in command of the blockading fleet, came ashore to watch the naval guns help pound the city. What he saw displeased him. He insisted that sailors, not soldiers, fire the naval cannons. Immediately the accuracy improved.

Disasters overwhelmed the Mexicans. The children of Vera Cruz were pathetic. In every minute of every hour the Americans had a shell in the air. Mexican strong points returned the fire, but Scott had his infantrymen in trenches. The night bombardment, with the sky streaked with red and the city in flames, was even more terrible. Buildings crashed and some caught fire. Smoke shrouded the city. The tragedy of war swept over the place like a fog from hell.

In the second day of the battering, foreign consuls inside the town sent word to Scott asking if the bombardment could cease so women, children, and neutrals could leave. This placed a hard decision up to the old general. If he agreed, it would obviously aid the enemy by giving him time and would consequently endanger his mission and his soldiers. He refused.

After four days, after "four or five hundred citizens and four hundred Mexican soldiers had perished," Morales, to save face, had his second-in-command surrender. The Americans had fired 6,700 projectiles into Vera Cruz—"The City of the True Cross." Church bells tolled for its dead.

About eighty Americans were wounded by Mexican shell-fire, and nineteen died.

---

* Brother of Commodore Oliver Hazard Perry, hero of the battle of Lake Erie in the War of 1812.

Scott permitted the Mexican soldiers to march out of the forlorn city with their side arms after they had given their word of honor to fight no more. Old Bruin and his sailors landed, marched into the dirty fortress, and raised the American flag.

Santa Anna, in permitting the Americans to land at Vera Cruz, had made a bad error.

To assist the Mexicans General Scott ordered his soldiers to help clean up the wreckage in the streets of Vera Cruz and to give the hungry people rations. He insisted on discipline. He would have none of the conduct that some of Taylor's soldiers had exhibited at Monterrey. When an American raped a Mexican woman, General Scott placed him before a court-martial and then carried out the court's sentence by hanging the criminal.

Scott's soldiers wanted to see the sights of the city. He permitted this, making them travel in small groups under an officer or a sergeant to insure they behaved. The general was anxious to impress the Mexicans. To show them he was friendly and that he respected their religion, he took his staff with him and attended Mass. Although not a Roman Catholic, he lighted a candle before the altar. The Mexicans did not know what to make of the towering, unpredictable general.

And perhaps many did not know about him in Washington. Vera Cruz had hardly surrendered when Scott was handed a letter from Secretary of War Marcy. It rebuked Scott for his part in the trial of Colonel Harney, the hot-headed officer who staged his own fatal invasion of Mexico and who had refused to obey orders. The reprimand came at the moment of victory, and Scott felt hurt.

He sat down and answered, and, as often when he was on the defensive, Scott took the offensive. In his reply, he un-

corked a long-winded sentence that was not too clear except
its ending: "I waive further reply, having, at the moment, no
inclination and no leisure for controversy." With all his problems, the reprimand seemed to the giant like a gnat's bite.

He assembled his hand-picked staff—"my little cabinet," he
called them. One was a young captain of Engineers from Virginia who had distinguished himself in his studies when he was
a West Point cadet. This was Robert E. Lee. In reporting on
the battle at Vera Cruz, Scott termed Lee "daring" and a
hard worker. Lee was coming into his own. People liked him,
not only because he was smart but because he had a relaxed
manner, and obviously Lee was becoming a most valuable
field soldier.

Scott discussed the bad transportation situation with his
staff. The general said he was not going to head inland on a
shoestring. Pack and wagon trains to carry supplies were a
necessity. So up and down the coast went expeditions to try
to buy mules. One foray had the help of the navy.

Winfield Scott worked his men to ready themselves for the
fight to the west. At times, when the atmosphere was clear,
the massive and beautiful mountain, Orizaba, appeared in the
west. It seemed to indicate not only the roughness of the
country but obstacles that lay ahead.*

* See Map No. 7, pages 134–135.

15   CERRO GORDO

Eleven days after the fall of Vera Cruz, Winfield Scott had enough animals to start about one fourth of his army toward Mexico City. His aggressive American force numbered about ten thousand men; he had to leave some on guard, and some were sick.

The first forty miles along the sandy coastal plain were hard. Hot and humid weather and a fast pace made many of the soldiers fall out. Hiking with pack, rations, ammunition, bayonet, and a heavy musket in such weather over a road that twisted upward into the hills was difficult. Every now and then the road dipped down into a rocky ravine, then wound back up hill. This was the path along which Cortés, the Spanish conqueror, traveled more than three hundred years before into central Mexico to subdue the Aztec empire. Once the road had been paved and guttered by Cortés' slaves, but now it was in bad shape.

Not far behind the advance guard trotted Old Davy the Bengal Tiger Twiggs. Scott ordered him to take the advance, and this laid the basis for trouble. Haughty Bill Worth felt that the honor of leading the army into enemy country belonged to him. He looked down on Twiggs, believing he had shirked at Monterrey. (It was just about a year before that they had quarreled over rank.)

Although Scott felt bad, because he realized his long friendship with Worth was being disrupted, he was not one to change such an order. Worth, probably even more sensitive than the senior general, had his feelings hurt, too. Worth could not accept what he considered a slight. He could not keep his bitter thoughts quiet, and this did not add to the teamwork in the army. He had named his only son after Scott, and he was starting to regret it.

In a few days after the departure of the advance division under Twiggs, there were enough white-canvas-topped baggage wagons so the rest of the army could move. Worth led his division out of Vera Cruz for the mountainous country on April 13, 1847.

Soon after leaving the coast, the soldiers hiked along the road bordering the immense estate of Santa Anna. For fifty miles his property stretched, slightly beyond the town of Jalapa.*

Scott was back at Vera Cruz checking on "wagons, medicines, hospital stores and some bacon" when exciting news broke. A squad of dragoons rode in with word that Captain

* See Map No. 7, pages 134–135.

Roberts' pack train with the paymaster's money had to pull back in a hurry. Santa Anna's soldiers had arrived and were blocking the road.

Scott, with all his marvelous attributes, was vain. He wrote later in his *Memoirs* under the heading, "Scott Called to the Front": "I left Vera Cruz . . . with a small escort of cavalry under Captain Philip Kearny and hastened to the front. When I arrived no commander was ever received with heartier cheers."

There were cheers, but the news was grave. Santa Anna, back from the north and now President of Mexico, because of his adroitness as a politician and because of his "victory" over Taylor at Buena Vista, had a position on hills bordering the main road near the village of Cerro Gordo.

With his boundless energy, SA had collected money from every possible source to pay his soldiers and buy supplies. Some of the beef herds for his men came from his own estate. He had twelve thousand soldiers with him—some veterans of Buena Vista, some untrained. When he and his army had marched for the north out of San Luis Potosí, his men wore gaudy uniforms. Now about half of them wore anything they could scrape up. White pantaloons seemed to be the most common garment for hundreds.

In hills near the village of Cerro Gordo, SA selected a defensive position and ordered his men to dig trenches. His chief engineer protested, pointing to the high cliff behind the main position. "If we are defeated," the engineer said, "our men will be trapped. They would be forced straight back down the road because that cliff blocks a possible retreat."

SA paid little or no attention. He was determined that the pass near Cerro Gordo would be the battlefield, and he ordered his cannons placed so they could rake the road and defend the hills. Although the fortifications were not completed when the Americans came, SA was content. He said, "Not even a rabbit can get through." He liked the place because if he stopped Scott's men here they would be in a valley where many would die from the cursed *vomito*.

While Scott and his cavalry escort were racing toward his soldiers near Cerro Gordo, Capt. Joseph E. Johnston of the Corps of Engineers and other scouts went on reconnaissance to find out more about the enemy. It was hard scouting along the stream beds because of the heavy jungle growth, and as they neared the Mexican outposts, shots zipped down the road. The scouts ducked for cover.

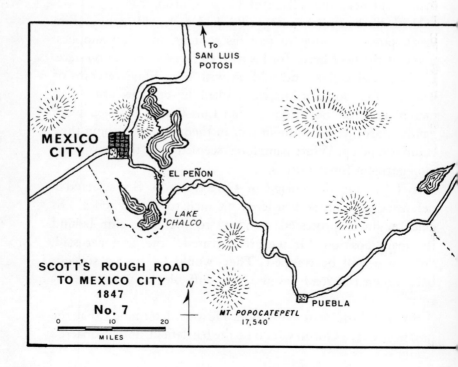

SCOTT'S ROUGH ROAD
TO MEXICO CITY
1847
No. 7

Occasionally they could hear a bugle call and the strike of a pick as the Mexicans worked to improve their defenses. Probably they were on Cerro Gordo—"Big Hill"—a volcanic cone rising out of the jungle about two hundred yards off the road. There was no noise to the left. There was a river over there. The enemy might be on adjacent hills. To make sure, Johnston exposed himself, and a bullet clipped him. His men carried him back to have his serious wound dressed.

One of Scott's first orders on arrival at the scene was to send out more engineer officers, including Capt. R. E. Lee and Lts. P. G. T. Beauregard and Zealous B. Tower. "I can't plan an attack," Scott said, "without information about the enemy. I want to know where he is and how strong he is."

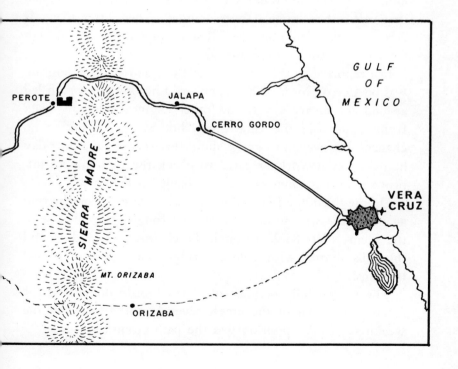

Scouting on his own, Lee found a trail. Because little sun could beat its way through the jungle growth between the brown hills, hundreds of muddy footprints showed in the path. Obviously men had walked over it recently. Lee followed it carefully—toward the enemy's lines. Then it veered to the north. He walked cautiously—he might be a target for a hidden outpost.

When he heard Spanish voices in the jungle, he ducked off the trail and hid behind a huge, vine-covered log near a spring. Here came a group of Mexicans to fill their canteens. Lying in the dank vines next to the log, Lee could not even brush ants off his face, neck, and arms without fear of being discovered. Some of the Mexicans sat on the log just above him. They were in no hurry to get back to their work. When they left, others came. Hours dragged. Then, after Lee was certain they had all gone, he fell and scraped his way through the darkness to Scott's headquarters.

Lee reported to the general that the enemy's main position was on Cerro Gordo. The captain said he thought a path led around the enemy's left, and other engineers coming back from scouts said the same thing, but Scott was taking no chances. He needed to know about that trail. So the next day he gave Lee a working party to check the path and to improve it so that cannons could be hauled over it.

On the third day Lee and his workers were out on the trail again. There was no doubt now; the rough trail cut around the enemy's left flank—through the chasms, over and around the hills dotted with palms, scrubby oak, and occasional banyans.

The brown hill northeast of Cerro Gordo dominated the scene. It rose out of the jungle seven hundred feet. But the weakness of SA's position was the path around it.

The American engineers, and infantry working under them, labored to improve the tortuous path. Scott did not wait for it to be finished. He started the attackers over the trail. Lt. U. S. Grant described the tremendous task of moving cannons and men over it in his *Personal Memoirs:*

[The trail went through] chasms . . . where the walls were so steep that men could barely climb them. . . . Artillery was let down the steep slopes by hand, the men engaging a strong rope to the rear axle and letting the guns down, a piece at a time . . . paying out the rope gradually. . . . In a like manner the guns were drawn up the opposite slopes.

About noon, the Mexicans heard Lee's men on the path. A Mexican force smashed into the workers and their infantry guards. Davy the Bengal Tiger Twiggs saw no use in waiting longer, and he smartly ordered his soldiers to go to the rescue of Captain Lee's party and to attack. This was April 17, 1847. The Battle of Cerro Gordo was under way. It started right for the Americans because of the bravery of Lee, other engineers, the infantry scouts, and because of old-fashioned American labor.

However, trouble developed. Although Twiggs was right in starting the fight, he upset Scott's plan by not following the trail around to the enemy's rear. Winfield Scott had planned to have Generals Shields and Worth follow Twiggs's men over this roundabout way.

But Twiggs divided his men and failed to get around the enemy. To make matters worse, General Pillow mismanaged his attack. He led his men on the wrong side of a ridge and three Mexican batteries chewed them up, Pillow himself receiving a nick in the arm. His men of the 2nd Tennessee Volunteers were furious with him because many of their best soldiers died.

Because of the cliffs and ravines, the crack of the rifles and the thunder of the cannons sounded and resounded. It seemed as if fifty thousand soldiers were locked in a death struggle instead of about nineteen thousand.

Fortunately for the United States, Brig. Gen. James Shields led his men over the right trail. Down the slope they dashed near the village of Cerro Gordo, trapping the Mexicans. In the fight, Shields fell badly wounded.*

As a result of his maneuver and because of the pressure Twiggs's soldiers placed on the Mexicans in front of them,

---

* Shields, born in Ireland, rose to Supreme Court justice in his state of Illinois. He won his brigadier general's star by political appointment, but he proved to be a valuable, skillful leader.

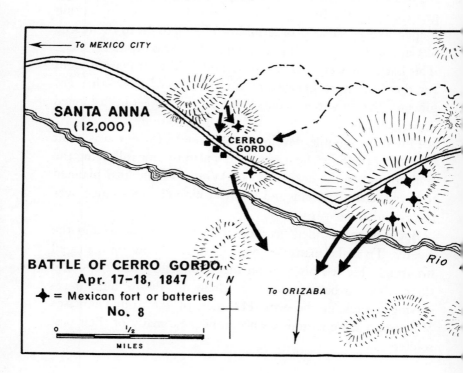

To MEXICO CITY

SANTA ANNA
(12,000)

CERRO
GORDO

BATTLE OF CERRO GORDO
Apr. 17-18, 1847
✦ = Mexican fort or batteries
No. 8

N

To ORIZABA

Rio

0   ½   1
MILES

Santa Anna's men fled from the battlefield. Rather than stick their heads into Shields's trap at the village of Cerro Gordo, numbers of them escaped by plunging into the rough country toward the town of Orizaba. The dictator himself was not a brave nor a determined defender. When he saw the Americans were winning, he galloped in the same direction as his fleeing men. His amputated leg was troubling him and he was almost spent, but he got away.

In the battle, three thousand of his men became prisoners, and Scott's soldiers gathered up hundreds of muskets and forty-three cannons. The prisoners posed a problem, because Scott could not spare soldiers to guard them. After some thought, he released the prisoners, making them swear to fight

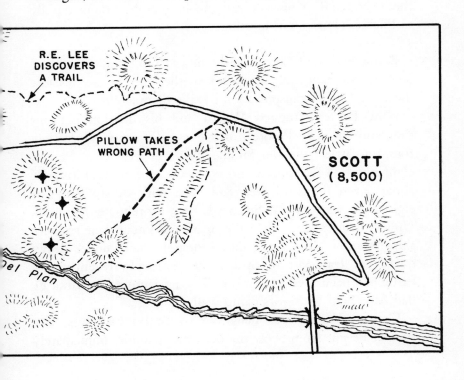

no more. No one knows how many of Santa Anna's men died or how many were wounded. The United States loss was thirty-seven killed and 337 wounded.

After the battle, there was nothing but praise for Capt. Robert Lee: He had performed splendidly. However, Lee felt terrible when he saw the dead and wounded. He wrote his father-in-law, George Washington P. Custis, "You have no idea what a horrible sight a battlefield is."

Gideon Pillow returned to the States for a short leave after the fight, and to the disgust of the 2nd Tennessee Volunteers —who had never liked him—the President promoted Pillow to major general.

On a ranch far to the south, SA managed to round up about three thousand of his soldiers, and he marched them rapidly to Puebla. He was not quitting.

Before Scott left Cerro Gordo, he ordered his men to throw most of the captured weapons into the river gorge, because the army lacked transportation to take them along.

Now he leap-frogged Worth and his division of four thousand ahead to Perote, forty-five miles away. Here they found a castle from the Middle Ages. The castle of Perote, eight hundred feet square, sitting in the hills at an altitude of about seven thousand feet, had been built of stone in the eighteenth century by Spaniards as a storehouse for gold. Under their system, when the Spaniards knew their treasure ships were at Vera Cruz, they sent gold there under heavy guard for transport to Spain. Comparatively recently, the castle had been used as a prison. Texans captured in Santa Fe had been held within its damp walls.

General Worth was delighted to be on his own. The further he got from Scott the better he liked it. Immediately after the Battle of Cerro Gordo, Worth had urged Scott to march at once to Mexico City, but there were difficulties and Worth refused to see them.

On the march, when the Americans passed a town, Mexicans, anxious to be friendly and to make money, came out of thatched huts and offered skinned pigs, fresh-water shrimp, pie, bananas, onions, sun-dried beef fried in peppers, hot *mole* (chili) sauce, turkeys, and *pulque*—available in gourd flasks and in animal skins. "Stay away from that fermented juice," the sergeants warned the privates. "Makes you drunk as four hundred rabbits."

The scenery along the volcanic road was picturesque. Although the days were warm for marching, you needed a blanket at night. To the left rose the ice-clad peaks of Popocatepetl and Iztaccihuatl, the "Smoking Mountain" and the "White Lady." * Sun on their slopes made the snows glisten. Scott's men labored on the road as it climbed through pine forests, past ranch country, then walked more easily as it slanted through the hills down into the beautiful town of Jalapa.

Scott and most of the army stopped here, just nine miles from the Cerro Gordo battlefield. This was April 19, 1847. On May 6, when he was farther into Mexico, Winfield Scott would put into action one of the strangest decisions a United States general ever made.

On the Mexican side, thousands of people took the defeat at Cerro Gordo as a terrible blow. Now more Mexicans saw the dictator in his true light—a cruel adventurer who could inspire people to follow him and who posed as a general. Not only had he outnumbered Scott at the Big Hill, but he had

* See Map No. 7, pages 134–135.

chosen the ground for the battle. The Mexican Congress could not make up its mind what to do about him. Although he was fast losing prestige and popularity, he was the best organizer in the country. In Mexico City, working to enlist men for its defense, was Nicolas Bravo, political general, but not everyone trusted *him;* he had once accepted a bribe. In the present chaos, Santa Anna stayed on as senior general and dictator—as well as an affliction for the Mexican nation.

16   DANGEROUS INTERLUDE

THE dictator's decision to beat Scott to Puebla was a bad one. Had SA remained on Scott's flank near Orizaba, Scott could not have considered advancing on the capital. He would have had to go into the wild country after the Mexican leader and his men. This was Santa Anna's fourth strategic mistake.*

The Mexican government found itself in a frightening position. If it went on with the war, there seemed to be no assurance of victory, and if it sued for peace, it risked anarchy from restless elements in the cities. One Mexican poet wrote:

> "Tortoises in the country,
> Vultures in the city."

* Others: abandoning Tampico, marching north to try to destroy Taylor, and permitting Scott to land at Vera Cruz.

While Santa Anna was working in Puebla to ready an army to face Scott again, he encouraged guerrilla warfare against Scott's supply line from Vera Cruz. The jungle lent itself to this type of fighting, but the guerrillas were not successful on a large scale. To overcome a supply train and its guards, they had to concentrate, hide, and strike when the time was right. Guerrilla leaders who could control as many as one hundred untrained men were hard to find. About all the guerrillas had done so far was to kill a few supply guards and to put pressure on the drivers and guards who came through unharmed. The guards of the trains had to be ready, at the first sign of ambush, to fire at least one aimed shot without delay in order to try to lessen the enemy's fire, then to take cover fast, locate the enemy, deploy, and fight. Santa Anna felt bad because first reports reaching him on guerrilla warfare said his irregulars usually ran away after they fired the initial volley. Nevertheless the guerrillas tormented the Americans and slowly became more effective.

While Santa Anna was in Puebla, he levied, to help his cause, a tax on "people who could stand it" and seized money belonging to the Academy of Fine Arts. He was surprised to find hundreds of citizens in Puebla who did not want to fight the *gringos*.

On the American side many things worried Winfield Scott. His principal concern, and it was a heavy cross, was that in a few weeks about 3,700 of his volunteers would arrive at the end of their enlistments. They would then be due to go home to the United States, and they wanted to go. Reducing his small army—in enemy country—was no way to secure victory.

Obviously the longer Scott delayed his march to Mexico City, the longer the Mexicans had to recover from Cerro Gordo.

He also felt anxious because the wagon trains from Vera Cruz were not large enough to haul supplies piling up there, and because he lacked cavalry enough to bring the trains through and at the same time punish the guerrillas.

Scott delayed nearly a month at Jalapa, waiting, as he termed it, "[for] our feeble trains, and without a faint hope of reinforcements. Not a company came." This was a blow. In spite of a bonus to reenlist, authorized by Congress, inquiry among the men due to go home disclosed that only one company of Tennessee cavalry would remain and fight. The fact that he had warned of the difficulty seven months back did not console him.

Scott considered his puzzle. With luck, he might capture the capital of Mexico in six to eight weeks. However, by that time yellow fever would be raging in Vera Cruz, and if the volunteers arrived there then, many would die. Scott wanted to win, but not that badly.

Winfield Scott possessed the strength of character to stop his drive into the heart of enemy country and to send the 3,700 men home. On May 6 they left under General Patterson for Vera Cruz.

The total number of American soldiers in the country of Mexico was now about six thousand.

The situation was unique in the history of modern warfare. Fortunately for the United States, the Mexicans were disorganized and could not attack Scott's soldiers.

Then one night forty US cavalrymen rode into Jalapa guarding a letter. It was from a Mr. Nicholas P. Trist, newly arrived from the United States. Trist had written his letter in Vera Cruz and said it was so important it must be delivered, without delay, to General Scott. The cavalrymen, impressed by Mr. Trist's credentials and his imperious manner, had agreed to ride at once with it to the general. It was bad enough to have forty cavalrymen ride through enemy country just to guard a letter, but when the general found that it was from the Chief Clerk of the War Department, who proved by the enclosure that he was a special agent sent to contact the Mexicans, Scott was furious. When General Scott became angry, it was not pleasant around headquarters.

The more Scott studied Trist's thirty-page, sarcastic, and irritating letter, the more exasperated he became. He was expected to pass on to the Mexicans a sealed letter from Trist without being 100 percent sure of its contents.

The general sprang for his pen and dashed off a forceful letter to Trist, lecturing him and telling him that "an armistice is a *military* question. . . ."

That Trist had been selected by President Polk and Secretary of War Marcy did not alter Scott's thinking. The general felt degraded, because *he* was the chief representative of the United States at this time in the war, and to have anyone else try to treat with the Mexicans for an armistice disregarded military custom and common sense.

Trist preached to the general in a lengthy letter, then violated protocol after arrival at headquarters by failing to call on the general. Things became ridiculous. Scott made sure his aide furnished Mr. Trist with a sentinel for protection, and the two corresponded with each other by letters instead of meeting face to face. They also wrote Washington. Back in the US capital, the President and the Secretary of War blamed Scott. They thought *he* should be nicknamed Haughty Bill.

In the meantime, Worth, under Scott's orders, marched into Puebla, brushing aside Santa Anna's cavalrymen. When SA pulled back to Mexico City, Worth marched his weary soldiers, four thousand of them, into Puebla, a town of eighty thousand. Fortunately, the large majority of the citizens did not favor the war.

Worth soon brought troubles on himself. He made terms with the city council, and then issued a circular to his soldiers warning them that "food for sale to you is purposely prepared to cause sickness and . . . death." The paper also said this was a familiar "Spanish trick . . . willingly practiced by the Mexicans." The fine citizens of Puebla rightfully felt insulted.

Into this broiling set of circumstances rode Winfield Scott. Trist was in his cavalcade, but they were not speaking.

The country they rode through was magnificent. Captain Roberts noted: "Mount Popocatepetl and Orizaba, magnificent sights, one covered with eternal snows. The conception [I had of them] was so feeble that I gaze on these everlasting heights with amazement. . . ."

General Worth met the commanding general outside Puebla and escorted him into the city with all the pomp he could command. A band on white horses furnished the music. Worth gave the general a banquet that night, but Scott was barely civil. In the morning he took steps that voided concessions Worth had made to the city council and had him withdraw his abusive letter.

When Scott worked to assure Mexican civilian leaders of the city that he did not believe for an instant in Worth's letter, Worth became furious. For a time, the number-one worry—the small number of American soldiers in Mexico—took a back seat. Worth asked for a court of inquiry, which recommended he be officially rebuked. "Probably," one historian says, "from this time on, Worth became a mortal enemy of Winfield Scott."

The only encouraging thing from a United States point of view was that when Trist became ill Scott, who was always anxious to bury the hatchet and end a quarrel, sent Trist a box of guava marmalade. This led to the two becoming friends, and they talked over their problems. Then both received letters from Washington correcting them. President Polk was unable to see that in sending Trist as a special envoy he had created an absurd situation.

In July, Mexicans came to Mr. Trist and said that if Santa Anna received one million dollars, with ten thousand dollars as a down payment, the war would stop at once. Immediately Scott called a council of war. He said he was for the idea and pointed to the buying of peace treaties from the Indians and to a deal with the Barbary pirates as precedents. He was strongly motivated by the thought that if the war ceased no more of his men would be killed or maimed in battle. He said stopping the war at a cost of a million would be a bargain. General Quitman argued the other way, saying bribery would be humiliating to the United States. Scott stood his ground and gave the Mexican envoys ten thousand dollars from a secret service fund. The rest of the money would come from a three-million-dollar appropriation from Congress.

The scheme blew up, SA quickly using the ten thousand dollar advance to strengthen the forts guarding the capital.

For three months Winfield Scott and his army cooled their heels, waiting for reinforcements to arrive in Puebla. Fortunately, because of Scott's diplomacy, Puebla was not nearly as hostile as it had been. He also managed to obtain food and clothing for his men in the city.

Finally replacements from the US hiked in on the coast road. Some were recruits, and they had a harsh introduction, because guerrillas caught them in the gauntlet. The guerrillas were fighting harder now, although they did let a large supply train of four hundred wagons and a thousand heavily loaded pack mules slip by near the end of May. Major General Pillow returned; this was hardly an encouragement for the Americans. One of the new arrivals, leading 2,500 men and a heavy train of siege guns, was Brig. Gen. Franklin Pierce. One day he would become President of the United States.

In Mexico City, Santa Anna was flitting in and out of the Presidency, making each move as dramatic as possible. The Mexican newspaper, *Monitor Republicano*, ridiculed him. It said he was making "the ultimate the very finalest... [move]." But, as distrusted as he was, Santa Anna managed to remain in the saddle as head of the government and as senior general of the army.

In the capital, his frenzied attitude was causing men in the foundries, in the powder mills, and in the army to labor long hours. Smart engineers were building forts to block the *gringos*. Even a leader who hated SA, General Gabriel Valencia, pledged his sword. The Mexicans' inherent love of country was giving the dictator 25,000 men.

In July and August, Scott received reports from many sources—newspapers, scouts, farmers, travelers, and spies—that Santa Anna's army was now "between 25,000 and 30,000."

One of the spies assisting Scott was Manuel Dominguez. Hitchcock labeled him "a helpful robber-chief." Dominguez, a natural leader and brave fighter, led his band of highwaymen and guerrillas over to the American side because he lost his robbery concession on the Vera Cruz–Mexico City road to rival bands sponsored by the government. After he swore eternal allegiance to the United States, Scott paid him three dollars a day, his men—who varied in number from 150 to three hundred—two dollars a day.

All sources told Scott that Santa Anna's force was growing

in size daily, that the defenses of the city were becoming more and more formidable.

Thousands of Scott's men were ill. Even though his army was small, he decided he must attack. Daringly, he cut loose from his base in Vera Cruz in order to gain men who were guarding his supply line. With audacity unsurpassed in modern times, he decided to go after the army of Santa Anna.

17   THE VALLEY OF MEXICO

WHEN Scott and his army of 10,738 soldiers marched
through the pass in the barrier of mountains, he knew
he had to continue to conserve the lives of his soldiers.

His capture of the City of the True Cross had cost the
lives of nineteen Americans. When news of the capture hit
New Orleans, it caused but a ripple of excitement as compared to the frenzy of emotion stirred by Taylor's victory at
Buena Vista. Later, in discussing the capture of Vera Cruz
and his disapproval of the suggestion that the town be taken
with the bayonet, Scott said, "If it had cost one hundred of
our soldiers, I would have felt like a butcher." Now at the rim
of the gorgeous valley, he realized that hard fighting lay
ahead; that many of his men would die.

It was unbelievable that Santa Anna permitted the American army to march so close to the city. Nineteen miles from the capital, Scott's men had a brush with an outpost and stopped, because behind the outpost the hill of El Peñon bristled with guns.

"We can take that hill," Scott said to his principal officers, "but we cannot afford its cost in lives."

Later, however, General Worth said that Scott wanted him and his division to smash straight into the death trap, directly at the hill.

Scott contemplated the various routes to the capital. He decided to move around Lake Chalco. Calling for Capt. Robert Lee and other Engineer officers, he sent them with armed escorts into the country far around the west side of the huge lake. Their mission was to search for the best roads—if there were any—trails at least, over which the cavalry could ride and the cannons and the ammunition and baggage trains could be hauled. The engineers and their escorts scouted thirty miles ahead of the army into dangerous territory.

To get away from El Peñon and to fool the enemy, General Scott had Twiggs's men march toward El Peñon as if they were going to attack the fortified hill. During this feint, Scott marched his army rapidly around the lake over trails the engineers had scouted, and arrived eight miles south of the city without the loss of a man. This was August 17, 1847.

Santa Anna was furious. He had ordered General Gabriel Valencia to defend each approach to the city, but Valencia hated the dictator so much he could not bring himself to obey orders. Now SA shifted his soldiers to block Scott.

Winfield Scott knew the eight miles to the city could be bloody ones.

On his scout, Captain Lee reached the tremendous area

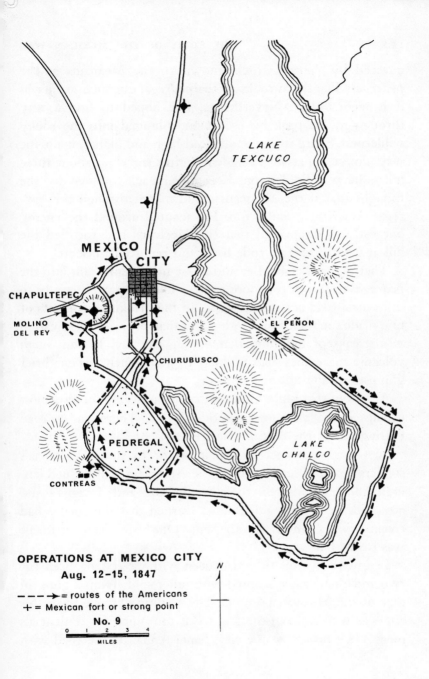

LAKE
TEXCUCO

MEXICO CITY

CHAPULTEPEC

MOLINO
DEL REY

EL PEÑON

CHURUBUSCO

PEDREGAL

LAKE
CHALCO

CONTREAS

OPERATIONS AT MEXICO CITY
Aug. 12–15, 1847

N

- - - -→ = routes of the Americans
+ = Mexican fort or strong point

No. 9

0 1 2 3 4
MILES

covered by volcanic rock known to the Mexicans as the *pedregal*. The sharp rocks of the *pedregal* cut shoe leather as if it were butter. Nevertheless, Lee hoped to find a way through it. He took his escort and plunged into the rocky wilderness. Sharp stones, some head-high and higher, made the way almost impassable. Suddenly, after traveling about three miles, he was fired upon. Lee pulled back, buoyed by the thought that if the Mexicans could march through the *pedregal* Americans could, too. He scouted around the enemy outpost and discovered that the Mexicans had fortified the hill at Contreras. Lee rode back and reported to Scott.

That night at eight, Lee and a few men went again into the *pedregal* to search for more routes. They hoped especially to discover a road across the waste. In the blackness, torrents of rain made the rocky forest gloomier than ever. Their salvation was streaks of lightning that cut up the sky. In the rough volcanic maze they had nothing to guide them except brief glimpses of the hill at Contreras.

At eleven that night Captain Lee, his powerful body almost exhausted, made his report in Scott's tent. There was no road cutting across the volcanic waste.

Scott had a chance to block off or to shield Valencia's soldiers from the main part of the American army. But General Pillow impulsively took his division and Twiggs's and attacked. Lee, now with Pillow, warned that the enemy had twenty-two cannons on the hill. One American regiment was tossed back.

Lee, who by this time had been without rest or sleep for two and a half days, scouted with other soldiers up a gully in rear of the Mexican position. The resulting attack from this angle as well as from the front was too much for Valencia's men. They broke for the city. Santa Anna, on the road with seven thousand of his soldiers, met the fugitives streaming for the capital. There was little SA could do now. He ordered his army, 25,000 strong, to take positions to defend the city's last lines of defense. It was to be a do-or-die fight.

At Contreras "fewer than one hundred Americans were killed or wounded. Seven hundred Mexicans died. . . ." The last was a guess—813 were taken prisoner. Seven hundred Mexican pack mules and stocks of ammunition and supplies as well as the twenty-two cannons were captured.

SA's force was scattered and in full retreat to their next position. After them stormed the Americans. Four miles from the city the Mexicans prepared to carry out Santa Anna's order: "Hold the Churubusco bridgehead at all costs."

Churubusco, the ancient Aztec word for "Place of the War God," fulfilled its meaning when the thunder of the guns began.

Without making a reconnaissance to find the best routes, Worth and Pillow ordered an attack. The Mexicans had a strong defensive position, their backs at the Churubusco River. It excited the Americans to see that one of the artillery battalions fighting for Mexico was the San Patricio Battalion of deserters. More than ever the Americans felt determined to succeed.

The deserters poured aimed fire at their former countrymen, and served their cannons as fast as they could, because they knew that if Mexico lost a hangman's noose or a well-placed bullet awaited them. The thunder of the cannonade shook the city.

After heavy losses that beat the Americans back, Worth's men crossed marshy ground and charged the Mexican position from the rear. Mexican resistance in the Churubusco position collapsed after a half day's fight. Colonel Harney, the same officer who caused Wool and Scott embarrassment, rode with his dragoons in a reckless pistol-and-saber attack to the very gates of the city. Coming back from this charge against the guns guarding the gate, Capt. Phil Kearny, daring leader and horseman, lost an arm to a rifle ball.

Sixty-six deserters of the San Patricio Battalion were captured—the last to show a white flag at Churubusco. They were a sad group. The British counsul-general, Mr. Macintosh, tried to intercede for them, but Scott thundered, "He who deserts to the enemy in time of war shall suffer death!" But his loyal soldiers knew the old general had a soft heart, and they said, "His bark is worse than his bite."

On the evening after the fight Winfield Scott, consulting with Nicholas Trist and hoping to end the war without having to crash into the city, called for an armistice. The Mexicans were happy to talk. In his *Memoirs*, at this point when things seemed to be breaking his way, Scott almost gloatingly returned to his awkward phrase "to conquer a peace."

The armistice between the two sides began on August 23, 1847. But the untrustworthy dictator used the lull to strengthen the defenses of the city, and when General Scott found this out he ended the armistice. It had lasted thirteen days.

Scott and his army were in a serious spot. On the map their position looked good; they were almost in the city. However, due to deaths, wounds, sickness, and the loss of men from the firing line because they had to be detailed as guards in the rear of the army, the American fighting forces were weaker by 3,558 than they had been seventeen days before, at the start of the battle at Contreras. As to the other side—"The enemy," Scott wrote, "[has] several times reënforced his line."

To solve the crucial problem of how to capture the capital,

Scott called a council of war. By its end he agreed with the majority of his generals: "Attack through the Molino del Rey and hit the walled castle of Chapultepec from the west." It seemed to be the best decision, but it was a grim one.

The Molino del Rey, the "King's Mill," once a cannon foundry, was a row of stone factory-type buildings stretching for two hundred yards. The dictator ordered sharpshooters stationed on their fortlike roofs. Nearby he placed four thousand cavalrymen, who would charge the Americans at the proper time.

In the two hours of fighting to capture Molino del Rey, Mexican sharpshooters cut down numbers of Worth's soldiers. When the Mexicans could no longer hold, they retired to Chapultepec.

This stone castle stood on an isolated hill, once the playground for the last of the Aztec emperors. Years later the Spaniards, near the end of the eighteenth century, built a castle here as a summer home for their viceroys. Now it was the site of the Chapultepec Military College as well as a fortress guarding the city's southwest approaches. Its very name had come to mean "unattackable."

General Scott called a council of war. "Gentlemen," he said to his leaders, "how are we going to capture the city?"

The majority favored the use of causeways, through the swamps on the south side.

Scott thought a while. "No, gentlemen," he said, "it will be Chapultepec. I am sure we can take it. It will hasten the end."

To try to mislead the defenders, Scott ordered some of his soldiers to attack the south side of the city. At dark these men were pulled back. American artillery thundered at the castle for a day and a half.

To capture Chapultepec, two divisions would storm straight ahead. In the first wave, Worth placed five hundred of his best fighters. Pen of the Army Hitchcock thought Worth had a bad idea in selecting these men because it weakened two regiments, separated officers from men, and destroyed regimental esprit. Hitchcock wrote later that Worth made the assault blindly. About seven thousand Americans were in this attack, three hundred of them being Marines in their first combat.

Here came the Americans. First the storming party, 250 strong, carrying ladders, axes, and crowbars. They crossed a ditch with their ladders, then rushed to place them against the walls. It looked like a scene out of the Crusades.

Mexican cannons answered the Americans. There was a moment when the assault hung in the balance. Some ladders were tossed back. To help the storming party, a lieutenant who all along had been brave in bringing his horse-drawn cannons close to the enemy again played a fearless part. This was Thomas Jonathan Jackson.

Jackson had been ordered to put his guns in front of the infantrymen. He dashed down the road toward the castle with his two cannons and their ammunition caissons, all horses at a gallop. At the ditch, he shouted commands that wheeled the horses and guns about. The gunners sprang to their places, loaded quickly, and fired. They had to fire accurately to help the American infantrymen. Mexican cannons answered Jackson's guns. One of his sergeants hesitated. In circumstances like this at Contreras, the battery's first lieutenant, John P. Johnstone, nephew of Joseph E. Johnston, had had his leg torn off, and cannoneers had been wounded, horses killed.

Jackson reassured the gunners by walking in front of the guns yelling, "There is no danger. *See! I am not hit!*"

Now he needed to get his guns closer. When some of his cannoneers were hit by grapeshot, Jackson helped surviving gunners carry one gun across the ditch where it could fire and help the assault. It was bravery, energy, and labor like this that put the Americans closer.

The soldiers, led by Pillow, Worth and Quitman, stormed in. The Mexicans fought bravely. At the top of the wall, hand-to-hand fighting began.

The fighting of the young cadets of Chapultepec Military College, wearing tasseled blue caps and blue full-dress coats ornamented with red collars and cuffs, was just as dramatic. Rather than surrender, six of the boys, aged thirteen to eighteen, died fighting. One wrapped himself in his country's flag and jumped to his death from the wall when the castle was about to be captured. The thought of being a prisoner was unthinkable to the noble cadets. For their gallant defense of the fortress the boys won the admiration and praise of the Americans.*

In contrast, the four thousand Mexican cavalrymen two miles away did not attack. Their leader said that a ravine kept them from coming to the aid of the defense. Why they did not leave their horses and fight on foot is not known. Mexican infantrymen, eight hundred of them, stationed outside the castle did not help the defenders inside Chapultepec to a great extent. Part of the defense lay in a carpet of mines outside the walls. Lieutenant Alemán, Mexican engineer whose duty it was to explode them, reported that the Mexican infantry

---

* One of the first lessons in Mexican history for young Mexicans of today is the patriotism and sacrifice of *Los Niños Héroes*, "The Boy Heroes." Today a marble monument at the foot of the hill near the main entrance of Chapultepec lists the names of the young cadets who died fighting for their country: Juan de la Barrera, Francisco Marquez, Fernando Montes de Oca, Agustin Melgar, Vicente Suarez, and Juan Escutia.

unintentionally blocked him from exploding the mines until it was too late.

`At the end of an hour the Americans held the castle. By this time both sides had paid a price. About 1,800 Mexicans were killed, wounded, or captured. The sad tallies included 811 Americans, of which 673 were wounded. Among those suffering from wounds was the young West Point engineer, R. E. Lee.

One of the leaders out front with a small detachment, scouting the way into the city from the west, was 2nd Lt. U. S. Grant. He was small, but the way he led men made him seem a giant.

Grant saw that to enter the city Mexican soldiers guarding the gate had to be dispersed. Then he ran across a platoon of Americans who were hoping to get close enough to scale the walls of the gate. They had a mountain howitzer, a small cannon.

Grant pointed out a church steeple nearby. He said to the officer with the howitzer, "Let's put the gun up in the belfry and shell the defenders. Come on!"

They took the gun apart, carried it up into the steeple, assembled the gun, and fired. The range was between two and three hundred yards. Grant and the soldiers serving the howitzer were in danger. They had no defenses other than this one gun. The fire from the gun drove the Mexicans from the gate.

American columns now chased Mexican soldiers through the town. Criminals in the city jails were freed at Santa Anna's order. They mingled with the *léperos*—untrustworthy members of the rabble—and street fighting broke out. When the *léperos* began to snipe at Americans, Worth was quick to place sharpshooters on the flat-top roofs. The city seemed worse than a cage full of crazy squirrels.

The place was hell. Terror increased. Santa Anna, seeing he had no chance, hurriedly left the city with part of his army. The people were not only resigned to their fate, but they were frightened.

The terrible street fighting reminded veterans of the battle of Monterrey of the blasts, confusion, and death that reigned during Old Rough and Ready's house-to-house fighting. When Scott heard that American soldiers were shot down in the capital, he became so angry that he swore he would level to the ground the block of houses from which the shots came.

In twenty-four hours, when the street fighting stopped, the Mexicans asked for terms. Scott insisted they surrender the city entirely. When this occurred he announced his terms: Rather than allow the soldiers to pillage at will, the city would be taxed, in accord with the times, a sum of $150,000. The citizens paid gladly. This money went to help the American sick and wounded and to start a fund to build the Old Soldiers' Home in Washington, D.C.

Early on the morning of September 14, 1847, the winning general made his soldiers think of his nickname, Old Fuss and Feathers. With an escort of dragoons, the giant—wearing his fore-and-aft hat and full-dress uniform with a gold sash, a huge sword hanging from his saddle—galloped into the Grand Plaza. The dramatic entry and the genuine cheers of his soldiers impressed the Mexicans. His men were already impressed. They knew that they had as a leader one of the best American generals of all time.

For two more days street fighting raged. Then Scott made it stop.

In a report to Mr. Marcy from the National Palace of Mexico, he wrote:

Sir:

At the end of another series of arduous and brilliant operations of more than forty-eight hours continuance, this glorious army hoisted, on the morning of the 14th, the Colors of the United States on the walls of this palace. . . .

Later, officers wrote about Sam Grant's bravery. One of the writers was Robert E. Lee.

On September 16 the dictator resigned the Presidency, but people who knew him best were not sure he was finished.

Scott, although he commanded but a few hundred over six thousand soldiers, was truly emperor of the city. The war against Mexico was over—but unfortunately there would still be shooting.

Serious troubles began. Quarrels started in the American high command, the most bitter arguments ever to rack the American Army.

There was also the problem of the deserters. Both officers and noncommissioned officers asked their seniors, "What will happen to the deserters we have captured?"

18   A GOLD MEDAL

Scott was "emperor" of the city, but he had a hard job bringing its life back to normal. When his soldiers walked about, gangs of *léperos* attacked them, robbed them, or killed them. The general stopped this by taking five hundred of his best soldiers, making them into military police, and detailing them to help the city police force.

Now he had the puzzle of the deserters. About 260 of them had fought against the United States at Churubusco. Numbers escaped, but Scott had somewhere between sixty-six and eighty penned up. "Give them a fair trial," he ordered.

Feeling against them was running high in American ranks. Not only had they deserted their flag, but they had opposed their former countrymen at Monterrey, Buena Vista, and

Contreras, and at their last stand they had fought like cornered tigers. Sgt. John Riley, one of the prisoners, was the object of special hatred because he had taught the Mexicans the latest principles of field artillery.

The trial was fair; a number were declared not guilty and released. The Mexican clergy tried to intercede on behalf of those convicted, but Scott said, "Carry out the sentences of the court."

Forty-nine were sentenced to hang and twelve were to receive "fifty lashes with a rawhide, well laid on the bare back, and branding with a red-hot iron with the letter *D* on the cheek." Of the rest, four were pardoned because they had been captured by the Mexicans and, although forced into the San Patricio Battalion, had refused to fight. One was pardoned because he was a recruit. Riley received special punishment. His cheek was branded, and fifty lashes were applied to his bare back while he stood with arms tied around a tree. His head was shaved, buttons were cut from his uniform, then he was drummed out of camp to "The Rogue's March." At the end of this short march, American guards picked him up and turned him over to a labor camp, where he was worked at hard labor as a convict as long as the army remained in Mexico.

Branding and lashing, barbaric today, were legitimate punishments in every army in the world in the midnineteenth century.

There were tense moments when the deserters sentenced to hang were forced to dig their graves and when they were placed on horseback or in wagons, the noose tied to the scaffolding and around their necks. For the group hanged near Chapultepec, Colonel Harney made sure they could see the Stars and Stripes flying from a castle flagpole, a symbol of the futility of their ill-chosen course. A chaplain read a prayer; then the horses were started.

To bring peace to the country, Scott gave his attention to guerrillas operating on the road to Vera Cruz. "Mexican citizens have a terrible horror of these Guerrillas," Captain Roberts wrote. The Americans detested them, too—not just because they struck like snakes, but in hunting them you had to ride hard miles over rough trails and plow through the brush.

Capt. Benjamin Roberts noted in his diary: "If I am to be killed in this country, I wish it to be in a fair and respectable fight. I can conceive no more inglorious Death than to die by the hand of some rascally Guerrillas." He went on to describe a before-daylight expedition against the bandits. "We moved against them with great *secrecy*." Surprise and speed won out. "We captured," Roberts wrote, "a large train of tobacco, 230 horses, 200 Lancers [and many weapons] as well as a Colonel of Guerrillas, and as his Lancers bore the black flag with the Death's head and crossbones with the motto 'No quarters,' he may find poor mercy from a court."

In addition to encouraging guerrilla action, Santa Anna tried to regain his old power. He had resigned the Presidency and had been defeated on every occasion, but he believed he could still win. The trouble was, his men kept deserting. Even with this handicap, and with but a small army, he attacked "the six hundred sick Yankees in Puebla." The six hundred sick Yankees fought back, about fifty being killed or wounded. Then the fight developed into a siege, Santa Anna hoping to starve the Americans into surrender.

Just before this, in mid-September, 1847, Brig. Gen. Jo Lane, veteran of Buena Vista, a front-line soldier, landed at Vera Cruz with reinforcements for Scott: soldiers from Indiana, Ohio, Massachusetts, and Texas. When SA's guerrillas brought word that Lane was on the road to Mexico City with 3,500 men, SA planned to ambush them at Huamantla, a village of about five thousand people, twenty miles north of Puebla.

Lane, marching toward the trap, put his Texas Rangers out in front as an advance guard. The Texas Devils, the Mexicans called the hated Rangers. Jogging along on their wiry ponies, the Rangers looked fierce. Some carried four pistols in addition to a sword and a rifle hanging from their saddles. One of the best Rangers was a curly-headed captain who affected a trim red beard and at times a bow tie. This was Sam Walker, popular fellow and a leader who had helped Old Rough and Ready Taylor.

When the Rangers spotted Mexican cavalry near the village, they drew sabers and charged. In the noisy, wild melee, Walker tumbled from his pony, a pistol wound in his chest. The Rangers suddenly realized they were almost surrounded, and Lane and those fortunate enough to be mounted retreated at a gallop to save their lives. Santa Anna watched from a church steeple.

When the Texas Rangers could return to the battlefield, they searched for Sam Walker. The tough Rangers burst into tears when they found their beloved leader, dead on the ground.

Three days later, October 12, 1847, General Lane fought his way into Puebla. This time he had artillery ready to batter the town and to back up his foot soldiers. After an hour's bombardment, the town surrendered. This defeat was too much for Santa Anna. He resigned again, but this time—at long last —he abdicated. Justin H. Smith, the historian, summed up as a principal reason for his failure: "He was a man who believed that a collection of men was an army."

While this was going on, efforts between the Mexican and the United States governments to arrange a peace treaty dragged into the late fall.

On December 10, Hitchcock wrote of a dinner party Scott gave for senior American officers in Mexico City, and of "a remarkable compliment" the old general paid to the United States Military Academy at West Point, New York. Scott raised his powerful frame from the table and toasted West Point. Later he gave his "fixed opinion" of the Military Academy officers:

I give it as my fixed opinion that but for our graduated cadets the war between the United States and Mexico might, and probably would, have lasted some four or five years, with, in its first half, more defeats than victories falling to our share, whereas in less than two campaigns we conquered a great country and a peace without the loss of a single battle or skirmish.

This tribute became part of "plebe knowledge" at the Military Academy, upperclassmen requiring new cadets to memorize it for well over a hundred years.

About this time, the hatred that had been simmering in Gens. William Worth and Gideon Pillow for Winfield Scott boiled over. Scott had no love for Pillow, and when the old general read Pillow's official report on the battle of Contreras, he felt slighted. Then, in two weeks, Scott accused Pillow of violating Army Regulations by taking two small cannons—public property—captured from the Mexicans at Chapultepec.

Worth now became the target of an angry order Scott published. It inferred that both Pillow and Worth had written letters to newspapers in the States giving the two writers "false credit" for victories in combat. Lieutenant Colonel Duncan, brave and outstanding artilleryman under Worth, said that he had written one of the letters. Scott promptly placed him under arrest. Worth was so upset that he changed the name of his son from Winfield Scott Worth to William Scott Worth.

The harsh charges and countercharges were placed before Polk in Washington. Scott was said to have been reckless in his plan of attack against Chapultepec. The President, who was anxious to humiliate Scott, said he felt that the general's temper and vanity were the cause of the "unfortunate collisions." The President ordered a court of inquiry to look into the matters.

Scott had had enough of President Polk—indeed. One of the cankers bothering the general was that Washington thought of him as having 30,000 soldiers. Actually, he had almost 25,-000, with 20,316 of them tied down by garrison duties at key points or unavailable because of illness. This left him a maneuverable "army" of but 4,500. It seemed ridiculous to Winfield Scott to tempt the fates by remaining in a hostile country with such a small number ready for emergencies. On February 2, 1848, he wrote his superior in Washington that Mr. Trist had been able to sign a treaty with the Mexican commissioners, and in the same letter Scott suggested that the army be withdrawn from Mexico as soon as possible and that he also be ordered home.

Polk, in his turn, had had enough of Scott—he might become a presidental candidate. Now President Polk leaped at the chance and ordered the general to turn over his army to Gen. William O. Butler. Winfield Scott was through in Mexico. Polk had succeeded in doing what Santa Anna could not do: make Scott leave Mexico.

Scott sailed for home feeling depressed and unappreciated. He looked forward only to seeing his family in Elizabeth,

New Jersey; he had not seen them in a year and a half. Suddenly, US citizens almost everywhere recognized what he had accomplished. One of the first was Daniel Webster, who extolled him on the floor of the Senate, saying, "Scott has performed the most brilliant campaign on recent military record." Congress voted him a gold medal and the official thanks of Congress, and Polk himself had to present the medal at the White House.

Americans thanked and praised Scott. The states of Louisiana, Kentucky, and New Jersey honored him. The Mexicans themselves realized his greatness, and influential Mexican citizens offered him several times the high position of president-dictator, with a bonus of $1,250,000. He declined.

The court of inquiry, ordered by President Polk to resolve the quarrel between Scott and Worth, Pillow and Duncan, met in Puebla, in New Orleans, and then in Frederick, Maryland. Scott was embarrassed to discover he was required to defend himself. Ramón Alcaraz, Mexican author said, "The conqueror of Mexico found himself brought like a criminal before a military court." Such was Scott's reward from Polk.

The record of the court was voluminous, requiring almost a thousand pieces of paper. The result, outside of humiliating Scott, could be called negative. Worth withdrew his charges against Scott. The President himself laid aside some of the charges against the participants. But the bickering continued, Pen of the Army Hitchcock becoming involved. Finally the long-drawn-out inquiry fizzled out, with Pillow acquitted.

The Treaty of Guadalupe Hidalgo, ending the war, was signed on February 2, 1848, in the tiny central Mexican town of that name. In the signing, Mr. Trist played an important part. Although Polk, in a fit of displeasure, had recalled him,

Nicholas Trist had remained to finish the job. His unusual ability to deal with the Mexicans was an important factor in the signing of the treaty.

In it, Mexico ceded Texas to the United States, with the Rio Grande as the boundary, as well as New Mexico, including the present states of Arizona, New Mexico, Utah, Nevada, a small corner of Wyoming, part of Colorado, and California. The United States paid the unpaid claims of Americans against Mexico, and agreed to pay the Mexican government $15 million.

At the close of the war people all over the world realized that General Winfield Scott had won it. *The New York Times,* a few years later, quoted the Duke of Wellington: "Scott's campaign was unsurpassed in military annals. He is the greatest living soldier."

Scott saw how to win, rode over obstacles, and conserved the lives of his soldiers while gaining victory.

No general in our history had as many outstanding, efficient, and daring officers as he had in the Mexican War. Men like General Worth, Lieutenant Jackson—and others too numerous to mention. Two of them especially, Grant and Lee, benefited by being exposed to General Scott's leadership and amazing audacity. They saw how he planned his campaigns boldly, yet based his tactics on careful reconnaissance. And both saw how he benefited from well-trained and well-led artillery.

As general-in-chief of the United States Army for thirteen more years, Scott made bitter enemies and strong friends. He saw the beginning of the Civil War. In 1862, with that terrible war still tearing the country apart, he retired after serving the nation fifty-five years.

At the beginning of the Civil War Scott had secured the almost isolated national capital and mobilized the Union forces. Too old and sick to take the field, he nevertheless developed for President Abraham Lincoln the strategy by which the Civil War would be won.

In late June, 1862, Mr. Samuel Sloan, railroad president, summering in Garrison, New York, received a mysterious telegram. It read: "PREPARE TO RECEIVE A BROTHER PRESIDENT." Sloan sought out General Scott, who was living at West Point, across the river from Garrison. Together they puzzled it out and decided that it referred to President Abraham Lincoln.

Mr. Sloan and the general waited for several hours at the Garrison railroad station. Finally, at three in the morning, a special train thundered up the track, and Mr. Lincoln stepped onto the platform.

The old general was agitated. His hand trembled as he shook Abraham Lincoln's hand, inquiring if something were wrong.

"My dear general," Lincoln said. "I am glad to see you. There's nothing wrong, I assure you. I have only come up to see and talk with you."

Together they crossed the Hudson on the ferry to West Point. What they talked about has never been fully revealed.

On Mr. Lincoln's return trip to Washington, an excited crowd cheered him in the Jersey City depot. "Speech!" the crowd yelled. In typical Lincoln banter, the President answered, according to *The Sun* of Baltimore, Maryland: "When birds and animals are looked at through a fog, they are seen to disadvantage, and so it might be with you, if I were to attempt to tell you why I went to see General Scott. ... Now, I can only remark, it had nothing whatever to do with making or unmaking any general in the country. (Laughter and applause.) ... The Secretary of War, you know, holds a pretty tight rein on the press, so they shall not tell more than they ought to, and I'm afraid that if I blab too much he might draw a tight rein on me. (Roars of laughter and long applause, during which the President retired to his special railroad car.)"

Undoubtedly President Lincoln consulted General Scott about the course of the Civil War.

In the Mexican War of 1846–48, the Mexican people suffered because their principal general was far beneath Winfield Scott in character and ability. Mexico had the terrible misfortune of following the generalship of a vulture—unserviceable, unproductive, and unworthy of her people.

On June 12, 1848, when General Butler rode out of the Mexican capital with the last American soldier, the dreadful event was over. Now the United States had to answer new problems.

Slavery did not flourish in the new areas the United States acquired, as many had predicted it would. Nevertheless debaters, poets, and writers among the abolitionists, fearing that this might happen, worked hard and skillfully to present their view of the war—a twisted narrative. Consequently the correct causes of the struggle, and the stories of its battles and leaders, have been obscured.

ACKNOWLEDGMENTS AND
BIBLIOGRAPHY

W HEN I look back after completing a book, I am startled by the number of individuals who, in one way or another, contributed. For me, writing a book is a multiperson undertaking.

Dort Darrah Reeder skillfully, efficiently, and patiently assisted me with this manuscript in numerous ways, and this includes long days at the typewriter overhauling the various revisions and her extremely valuable suggestions.

I also thank Dr. Eugene O. Porter, professor at Texas Western College of the University of Texas at El Paso, for reviewing Chapters 3, 4, and 5. These chapters, dealing with the causes and background of the war, benefited by his studious and careful review.

Col. John Elting, who contributed to other books of this series, made available his unusual knowledge of American history and reviewed parts of this manuscript. His guidance is invaluable.

Mr. Egon Weiss, librarian at the United States Military Academy, West Point, New York, encouraged me and made source material available. Members of his staff also interested themselves in this work and assisted, particularly Mr. William Kerr, Mr. J. Thomas Russell, Miss Nancy Harlow, Miss Charlotte Snyder, Mr. Robert Bidwell, Miss Irene Feith, Miss Frances Lum, and Miss Theresa Toborski. Mrs. Alice Ponton helped me to gain a Mexican viewpoint by translating documents written in Spanish.

Mr. Gerald C. Stowe, curator of the West Point Museum, and Mrs. Jacqueline R. Espy, curator of the Alamo, supplied details for parts of the story.

I also appreciate the help of Lt. Gen. B. M. Bryan, Mr. Joseph R. Carroll, Gen. M. B. Ridgway, Col. E. "Van" Sutherland, Brig. Gen. Jack Whitelaw, and Lt. Col. William J. Livsey, Jr.

I thank individuals and publishers for permission to quote from the following books: *Campaign Sketches of the War with Mexico* by Capt. W. S. Henry, New York, Harper and Bros., 1848; *The Life and Letters of George Gordon Meade*, Vol. I, New York, Charles Scribner's Sons, 1913; *The Mexican War Diary of General George B. McClellan*, edited by William S. Myers, Princeton, New Jersey, Princeton University Press, 1917; *The Diary of James K. Polk*, 4 vols., edited by Milo Milton Quaife, Chicago, A. C. McClurg & Co., 1910; *To Mexico with Scott—Letters of Captain E. Kirby Smith to His Wife*, Cambridge, Massachusetts, Harvard University Press, 1917; *General William Jenkins Worth* by Edward Secomb Wallace, Dallas, Texas, Southern Methodist Press, 1953; and *The Texas Rangers* by Walter Prescott Webb, Austin, Texas, University of Texas Press, 1935.

I also found most helpful: the unpublished "Diary Kept During the Mexican War, November 24, 1846, to July 1, 1848" by Captain Benjamin S. Roberts, typewritten manuscript, U.S.M.A. Library, West Point, New York; *The 1820 Journal of Stephen Watts Kearny*, Valentine Mott Porter, editor, published in St. Louis by the Missouri Historical Collections, Vol. III, 1908; and the writings of José Fernando Ramírez, *Mexico During the War with the United States*, Walter V. Scholes, editor, translated by Elliott B. Scherr, Vol. XXIII, No. 1, The University of Missouri Studies, 1950, Columbia, Missouri, The University of Missouri Press, 1951.

I benefited, too, by referring to the following books and documents:

Alcaraz, Ramón and others, *The Other Side*, Colonel Albert C. Ramsey, translator and editor. New York, John Wiley, 1850.

American Military History, 1607–1953, Department of the Army. Washington, D.C., U.S. Government Printing Office, 1956.

Athearn, Robert G., *War with Mexico*. New York, Dell Publishing Co., Inc., 1963, for American Heritage.

Battles and Leaders of the Civil War, Vol. II. New York, The Century Co., 1888.

Baylies, Francis, *Major General Wool's Campaign in Mexico*. Albany, New York, Little & Co., 1851.

Beasley, Norman, *Texas: The Lone Star State*. New York, Doubleday, Doran & Co., 1936.

Brooks, Nathan C., *A Complete History of the Mexican War*. Philadelphia, Grigg, Elliot & Co., 1849.

Callcott, Wilfrid Hardy, *Santa Anna*. Norman, Oklahoma, University of Oklahoma Press, 1936.

Carleton, James Henry, *The Battle of Buena Vista*. New York, Harper & Bros., 1848.

Chambers, Lenoir, *Stonewall Jackson*, Vol. I. New York, William Morrow & Co., 1959.

Claiborne, John Francis Hamtramck, *John A. Quitman*, Vol. I. New York, Harper & Bros., 1860.

Clark, Joseph L. and Linder, Dorothy A., *The Story of Texas*. Boston, D. C. Heath & Co., 1963.

Clarke, Dwight L., *Stephen Watts Kearny, Soldier of the West.* Norman, Oklahoma, University of Oklahoma Press, 1961.

Coit, Margaret L., and the editors of *Life, The Sweep Westward,* Vol. IV, *1829–1849.* New York, Time Inc., 1963.

Commager, Henry Steele, and Allan Nevins, *The Heritage of America.* Boston, Little, Brown & Co., 1939.

Connelley, William Elsey, *Doniphan's Expedition and the Conquest of New Mexico—Containing a Reprint of the Work of Col. John T. Hughes (1848).* Kansas City, Missouri, Bryant & Douglas Book & Stationery Co., 1907.

Cooke, Philip St. George, *The Conquest of New Mexico and California in 1846–1848.* Chicago, The Rio Grande Press Inc., 1964.

Cutts, James Madison, *The Conquest of California and New Mexico.* Philadelphia, Carey & Hart, 1855.

DeVoto, Bernard, *The Year of Decision, 1846.* Boston, Houghton Mifflin Co., 1950.

Downey, Fairfax, "Tragic Story of the San Patricio Battalion," *American Heritage,* Vol VI, No. 4 (June 1955).

Elliott, Charles Winslow, *Winfield Scott: The Soldier and the Man.* New York, The Macmillan Company, 1937.

Esposito, Vincent J., Chief Editor, *The West Point Atlas of American Wars,* Vol. I. New York, Frederick A. Praeger, 1959.

Executive Document No. 60, 30th Congress, 1st Session, 1847.

Executive Documents, 28th Congress, 1st Session (1843–1844), Doc. No. 2.

Flanagan, Sue, *Sam Houston's Texas.* Austin, Texas, University of Texas Press, 1964.

Foreman, Grant, *Pioneer Days in the Early Southwest.* Cleveland, Ohio, The Arthur H. Clark Co., 1926.

Freeman, Douglas Southall, *Lee.* New York, Charles Scribner's Sons, 1961.

French, Samuel G., *Two Wars: An Autobiography.* Nashville, Tennessee, Confederate Veteran, 1901.

Frost, John, *Pictorial History of Mexico and the Mexican War.* Philadelphia, Thomas, Cowperthwait & Co., 1849.

Grant, U. S., *Personal Memoirs*. New York, Charles L. Webster Co., 1894.

Hamill, Hugh M., "Experiment in International Living." *National Geographic Mazazine*, Vol. CIII, No. 3 (March 1953).

Hanighen, Frank Cleary, *Santa Anna*. New York, Coward-McCann, Inc., 1934.

Henry, Robert Selph, *The Story of the Mexican War*. Indianapolis, Indiana, The Bobbs-Merrill Co., 1950.

Hicks, John D., *The American Nation*, Vol. I. Boston, Houghton Mifflin Co., 1958.

Hitchcock, Ethan Allen, *Fifty Years in Camp and Field*, W. A. Croffut, editor. New York, G. P. Putnam's Sons, 1909.

Hogan, William Ransom, *The Texas Republic*. Norman, Oklahoma, University of Oklahoma Press, 1946.

Hopkins, G. T., "The San Patricio Battalion in the Mexican War." *Journal of the U.S. Cavalry Association*, Vol. XXIV, No. 98 (Sept. 1913), pp. 279–284.

Houston, Andrew Jackson, *The San Jacinto Campaign*. Gulfport, Texas, 1925.

James, Marquis, *The Raven: A Biography of Sam Houston*. Indianapolis, Indiana, The Bobbs-Merrill Co., 1929.

Kane, Harnett Thomas, *Natchez on the Mississippi*. New York, William Morrow & Co., 1947.

Life of General Scott. New York, C. A. Alvord, printer (no date).

McCall, George Archibald, 1803–1868, U.S.M.A. 1822, "Letter to Captain Bradford R. Alden, describing the battle of Resaca de la Palma in the Mexican War, 1846. Camp at Matamors, June 1846."

McConnell, Joseph Carroll, *The West Texas Frontier*. Jacksboro, Texas, Gazette Print., 1933.

McCormac, Eugene Irving, *James K. Polk: A Political Biography*. New York, Russell & Russell, Inc., 1922 and 1965.

Memoirs of Lieutenant General Winfield Scott, 2 vols. New York, Sheldon & Co., 1864.

Miers, Earl Schenck, *The Great Rebellion*. Cleveland, Ohio, The World Publishing Co., 1958.

Military Uniforms in America. Washington, D.C., The Company of Military Collectors & Historians, 1949–1951.

Morison, Samuel Eliot, *The Oxford History of the American People.* New York, Oxford University Press, 1965.

Myers, John Myers, *The Alamo.* New York, E. P. Dutton & Co., 1948.

Nebel, Carl, and George Wilkins Kendall, *The War Between the United States and Mexico, Illustrated.* New York, D. Appleton & Co., 1851.

Nichols, Edward J., *Zach Taylor's Little Army.* New York, Doubleday & Co., Inc., 1963.

Niles' National Register, Jeremiah Hughes, editor. Vol. 71.

Owen, Charles H., *The Justice of the Mexican War.* New York, G. P. Putnam's Sons, 1908.

Parkes, Henry Bamford, *A History of Mexico.* Boston, Houghton Mifflin Co., 1960.

Public Document No. 378, 29th Congress, 1st Session.

Reid, Samuel C., *The Scouting Expeditions of McCulloch's Texas Rangers.* Philadelphia, G. B. Zieber & Co., 1848.

Ridgway, Matthew B., *Soldier.* New York, Harper & Bros., 1956.

Roa Bárcena, Jose María, *Recuerdos de la invasion norteamericana, 1846–1848.* Mexico, Buxo, 1883.

Robinson, Fayette, *Army of the United States with Biographies of Distinguished Officers of All Grades.* Philadelphia, E. H. Butler & Co., 1848.

Samson, William H. (editor), *The Letters of Zachary Taylor from the Battlefields of the Mexican War.* Rochester, N.Y., 1908.

Santa-Anna, Antonio López de, *The Mexican Side of the Texas Revolution.* Dallas, Texas, P. L. Turner Co., 1928.

Scott, Florence Johnson, *Old Rough and Ready on the Rio Grande.* San Antonio, Texas, The Naylor Co., 1935.

Semmes, Raphael, *Service Afloat and Ashore During the Mexican War.* Cincinnati, Ohio, William H. Moore & Co., 1851.

Singletary, Otis A., *The Mexican War.* Chicago, University of Chicago Press, 1960.

Smith, Arthur Douglas Howden, *Old Fuss and Feathers*. New York, The Greystone Press, 1937.

Smith, Justin Harvey, *The Annexation of Texas*. New York, The Baker & Taylor Co., 1911.

—— *The War with Mexico*, 2 vols. New York, The Macmillan Company, 1919.

Sowell, A. J., *Rangers and Pioneers of Texas*. San Antonio, Texas, Shepard Bros., 1884.

Steele, Matthew Forney, *American Campaigns*, 2 vols. Washington, D.C., Byron S. Adams, 1909.

Stephenson, Nathaniel W., *Texas and the Mexican War*. New Haven, Connecticut, Yale University Press, 1921.

Talbert, Frank X., *The Day of San Jacinto*. New York, McGraw-Hill Book Co., Inc., 1959.

Taylor, Zachary, *Letters of Zachary Taylor*. New York, The Genesee Press, 1908.

The Mexican War and Its Heroes. Philadelphia, Lippincott, Grambo & Co., 1854.

The Rough and Ready Annual or Military Souvenir, illustrated. New York, Appleton, 1848.

The Ulysses S. Grant Association, *Newsletter*, Vol. IV, No. 2 (January, 1967). Carbondale, Illinois, Southern Illinois University.

Wilhelm, Thomas, *History of the 8th U.S. Infantry from Its Organization in 1838*, 2 vols. Headquarters, 8th Infantry, 1873.

Williams, Alfred Mason, *Sam Houston and the War of Independence in Texas*. Boston, Houghton, Mifflin Co., 1893.

"Worth's Report." *Sen. Ex. Doc. No. 4* (Sept. 28, 1846), *29th Congress, 2nd Session, Vol. I*.

Zavala, Adina de, *The Alamo*. San Antonio, Texas, The Naylor Co., 1956.

INDEX

181